# NEW DIRECTIONS FOR CHILD AND ADOLESCENT DEVELOPMENT

William Damon, *Stanford University*
*EDITOR-IN-CHIEF*

# Variability in the Social Construction of the Child

Sara Harkness
*University of Connecticut*

Catherine Raeff
*Indiana University of Pennsylvania*

Charles M. Super
*University of Connecticut*

*EDITORS*

Number 87, Spring 2000

JOSSEY-BASS PUBLISHERS
San Francisco

VARIABILITY IN THE SOCIAL CONSTRUCTION OF THE CHILD
*Sara Harkness, Catherine Raeff, Charles M. Super* (eds.)
New Directions for Child and Adolescent Development, no. 87
*William Damon,* Editor-in-Chief

Microfilm copies of issues and articles are available in 16mm and 35mm, as well as microfiche in 105mm, through University Microfilms Inc., 300 North Zeeb Road, Ann Arbor, Michigan 48106-1346.

ISSN 1520-3247      ISBN 0-7879-5506-X

NEW DIRECTIONS FOR CHILD AND ADOLESCENT DEVELOPMENT is part of The Jossey-Bass Education Series and is published quarterly by Jossey-Bass Inc., Publishers, 350 Sansome Street, San Francisco, California 94104-1342. Periodicals postage paid at San Francisco, California, and at additional mailing offices. Postmaster: Send address changes to New Directions for Child and Adolescent Development, Jossey-Bass Inc., Publishers, 350 Sansome Street, San Francisco, California 94104-1342.

*New Directions for Child and Adolescent Development* is indexed in Biosciences Information Service, Current Index to Journals in Education (ERIC), Psychological Abstracts, and Sociological Abstracts.

SUBSCRIPTIONS cost $67.00 for individuals and $115.00 for institutions, agencies, and libraries.

EDITORIAL CORRESPONDENCE should be sent to the Editor-in-Chief, William Damon, Stanford Center on Adolescence, Cypress Building C, Stanford University, Stanford, California 94305-4145.

Cover photograph by Wernher Krutein/PHOTOVAULT © 1990.

Jossey-Bass Web address: www.josseybass.com

Printed in the United States of America on acid-free recycled paper containing 100 percent recovered waste paper, of which at least 20 percent is postconsumer waste.

# CONTENTS

# EDITORS' NOTES

Following William Kessen's discovery of "the American child and other cultural inventions" (1979), there has been growing recognition in the field of developmental psychology that conceptualizations of the child are socially constructed. As such, ideas about children—especially those held by parents and others who are directly concerned—vary widely but are nevertheless shared within communities (Harkness and Super, 1996). Although variability in ideas and practices related to children is a traditional focus of anthropology, the concept of socially organized individual differences in thinking presents new challenges for the field of developmental psychology. Three sets of questions are key to progress in this area:

- What is the nature of variability in ideas about children? Can variability best be conceptualized in terms of universal categories, such as individualism versus collectivism, or independence versus interdependence? Or is each socially constructed concept of the child unique, defying organization into such categories?
- At what social level can commonalities and differences usefully be identified? At the global level, differentiating between West and East? At the level of the society, measuring differences between cultural groups, social classes, or groups defined by educational background? Or at the level of the community, focusing on variability based on social roles?
- How is variability in the socially constructed image of the child expressed in interpretations of reality and in action in specific contexts? What happens when people with differing images try to communicate with each other about particular children?

The six chapters in this volume address these questions through studies of parents and others in a variety of cultural contexts. The theme of individualism versus collectivism (or independence versus interdependence) is discussed in all but one of the chapters, offering a greater appreciation of both the strength and the complexity of this concept as it applies to particular cultures. Harwood, Schölmerich, and Schulze use the constructs of individualism and collectivism to analyze relationships between cultural and social-class-based variability in their study of Puerto Rican and Anglo American mothers' long-term socialization goals for their children. Killen and Wainryb draw from research in three societies (Japan, Colombia, and the Druze culture of Israel) to critique universalist conceptualizations of independence and interdependence, showing how, contrary to the universalist view, both orientations are coexisting dimensions of development in a variety of cultures. The chapter by Raeff,

1

Greenfield, and Quiroz conceptualizes individualism and collectivism as historically constituted value systems that have varied implications for both independent and interdependent functioning, in this case for European American and Latino teachers, parents, and children. In another chapter, Greenfield, Quiroz, and Raeff analyze how individualistic and collectivistic images of the child appear to play a role in cross-cultural parent-teacher conferences. Harkness, Super, and van Tijen use these constructs to analyze cross-cultural differences between American and Dutch parents' descriptions of their children. Finally, although not focused on the individualism-collectivism dichotomy, the chapter by Seifert presents intriguing evidence on intracultural variability in concepts of the child.

As is evident, variability in the social construction of the child is analyzed here at many levels, from Harkness, Super, and van Tijen's challenge to the supposed unity of the "Western mind" to Seifert's comparison of differences among teachers, parents, and college students from the same cultural community. Harwood, Schölmerich, and Schulze propose that cultural communities should be viewed not as bounded, static entities but, rather, as groups of individuals who coconstruct a shared reality in one or more domains of life; they suggest that a primary focus of research interest should be the shared levels of discourse and practice among members of any such group. The usefulness of this perspective is illustrated in their analyses of differences in maternal behavior in several culturally scripted activities, such as infant feeding and mother-infant play.

The importance of culturally shared ideas for the formulation of plans for action is also demonstrated in Raeff, Greenfield, and Quiroz's analysis of European American and Latino parents', teachers', and children's responses to scenarios involving interpersonal dilemmas at home and at school. In general, the European American respondents favor solutions based on individual choices and consent, whereas the Latino respondents suggest resolutions based on the idea of automatic responsibilities and the promotion of group welfare. Similar differences are also highlighted in communication problems that European American teachers and Latino parents encounter in the context of parent-teacher conferences, as Greenfield, Quiroz, and Raeff show.

The social construction of the child, as a concept, has matured rapidly since its introduction to developmental psychology two decades ago. Understanding variability in the social construction of the child, as this volume proposes, is key to interpreting the relationships between thought and action in a wide variety of contexts.

Sara Harkness
Catherine Raeff
Charles M. Super
Editors

## References

Harkness, S., and Super, C. M. (eds.). *Parents' Cultural Belief Systems: Their Origins, Expressions, and Consequences.* New York: Guilford Press, 1996.

Kessen, W. "The American Child and Other Cultural Inventions." *American Psychologist,* 1979, *34,* 815–820.

*SARA HARKNESS is professor in the School of Family Studies and director of the Center for the Study of Culture, Health, and Human Development at the University of Connecticut.*

*CATHERINE RAEFF is a former postdoctoral fellow in applied developmental psychology at the University of California, Los Angeles. She is now assistant professor of psychology at Indiana University of Pennsylvania.*

*CHARLES M. SUPER is professor and dean in the School of Family Studies at the University of Connecticut.*

**1**

*In this chapter, we propose that the individualistic-collectivistic construct ignores cultural complexities, and we illustrate our points by using examples from our empirical research conducted in Japan, Colombia, and the Middle East.*

# Independence and Interdependence in Diverse Cultural Contexts

*Melanie Killen, Cecilia Wainryb*

Culture is commonly deemed central to analyses of social development. Very often, culture occupies *the* central role in explanations of social development, as it is assumed that the social development of individuals is, for the most part, determined by cultural forces and influences. One common conceptualization of the relation between culture and social development is based on the assumption that cultures form coherent and integrated systems of meanings and practices that can be characterized as either individualistic or collectivistic and that are explicitly or implicitly communicated through processes of enculturation, socialization, or social communication (Hofstede, 1980; Hsu, 1983; Markus and Kitayama, 1991; Triandis, 1995). The conditions under which any given culture develops individualistic or collectivistic orientations have not been the focus of much study and have usually been explained in reference to a variety of ecological and economic dimensions, such as cultural tightness, cultural complexity, societal size, subsistence level, and national wealth (see, for example, Berry, 1994; Kim and others, 1994; Triandis, 1995).

The lion's share of both theorizing and research using this perspective has been on the attributes of individualistic and collectivistic cultures and on the consequences of individualism-collectivism for the development of individuals and their interpersonal and intergroup relations. In general, cultures with an individualistic orientation are said to value the person as detached from relationships and from the community, as independent from the social order, and as motivated to attain personal goals. By contrast, collectivistic cultures value individuals according to their interdependent roles in the social system. Because individual social development is presumed to

NEW DIRECTIONS FOR CHILD AND ADOLESCENT DEVELOPMENT, no. 87, Spring 2000 © Jossey-Bass Publishers consist of the acquisition of the main cultural orientation, individuals in a culture are thought to acquire coherent, global characteristics that correspond to the unitary orientation of the culture (Shweder and Bourne, 1982; Triandis, 1995).[1]

During the past fifteen years, the construct of individualism-collectivism (I-C) has gained tremendous popularity as a predictive and explanatory model of variability in human thought, emotion, and behavior, and has generated a great deal of research across many cultures and across a wide array of domains (for overviews, see Kagitçibasi and Berry, 1989; Triandis, 1995). Indeed, some have suggested that the 1990s might be characterized as "the decade of individualism/collectivism" (Kagitçibasi and Berry, 1989; Kim and others, 1994).

However, the status of individualism-collectivism as a *dichotomous* construct is under scrutiny, even among I-C theorists. Triandis (1995, p. 42), for example, suggested that individualistic and collectivistic tendencies "can coexist and are simply emphasized more or less in each culture." It is possible that this statement reflects an attempt at revising the construct in response to criticisms (which are discussed further on). Nevertheless, Triandis's application of the I-C distinction remains squarely within the dichotomous framework, and the ensuing conceptualizations of the social and emotional lives of individuals in cultures remain unidimensional. As an example, in one of his most recent descriptions of individualism and collectivism, Triandis (1995, pp. 68–79) stated that members of individualistic cultures "base their identity on what they own" (p. 71) and display "ego-focused emotions" (p. 72), whereas members of collectivistic cultures base their identity on their group membership (p. 71) and display "other-focused emotions" (p. 71). In Triandis's view, the basic motivational structure of individualists "reflects their internal needs, rights, and capacities" (p. 72), but the motive structure of collectivists "reflects receptivity and adjustment to the needs of others" (p. 72). Individualists—Triandis argues—believe in self-reliance, hedonism, competition, and emotional detachment; collectivists favor attitudes that reflect sociability, interdependence, and family integrity (p. 73). Individualists value curiosity, creativity, and an exciting lifestyle; collectivists prefer security, social order, respect for tradition, and politeness (p. 74). Individualists emphasize abstract moral principles and rights, whereas collectivists focus on adherence to rules (p. 77).

It is likely that the use of dichotomous constructs as a conceptual or research heuristic remains popular because such simple constructs conveniently subsume complex and varied parameters and differences in a single dimension. However, when societies and individuals are pigeonholed into dichotomous categories, complexities and subtle differences are overlooked. Inevitably, the result is overly simplistic and distorted depictions of complex social realities (Mednick, 1989; Overton, 1998).

The dichotomy between individualism and collectivism has indeed fallen under heavy criticism (Killen, 1997; Sinha and Tripathi, 1994; Spiro,

1993; Turiel, 1994, 1998; Turiel and Wainryb, 1994; Wainryb, 1997; Wainryb and Turiel, 1995). Interestingly, the well-known anthropologist Clifford Geertz (1994, p. 3), once a proponent of the I-C distinction, recently argued that "descriptive reports of 'organic' societies governed by 'integrated' cultures, settled shapes, and solidified structures 'real as seashells,' grow unpersuasive. Stark 'great divide' contrasts between 'modern' and 'premodern' societies, the one individualistic, rational, and free of tradition, the other collectivistic, intuitive, and mired in it, look increasingly mythical, summary, and simple-minded."

In our view, the individualism-collectivism dichotomy results in the mislabeling of both cultures and individuals. Cultures and individuals are stereotyped in that they are described as supporting either an individualistic or a collectivistic ethos, without regard for other values or ideologies that may be part of the public or individual discourse. In this chapter, we discuss ways in which individualistic concerns with independence and collectivistic concerns with interdependence coexist in Western and non-Western cultures. First, we outline a theoretical framework explaining the coexistence of diverse social orientations in cultures and in individuals. Next, we illustrate such a coexistence with data drawn from our research programs in Japan and Colombia (Killen) and the Middle East (Wainryb).

## Cultural Ideologies and the Typing of Individuals

The notion that a "national character" or "cultural ethos" can be described in unidimensional terms has been in dispute for some time. In spite of the many characterizations of American society in terms of its deep commitment to individualism, social scientists have called into question the prevalence of individualism as a central idealized value in Western cultures. Some (for example, Fromm, 1941; Mills, 1956; Reisman, Glazer, and Denney, 1953; Whyte, 1956) have described Americans in nonindividualistic terms, emphasizing individual conformity to social norms and subordination to societal systems. Others (such as Bellah and others, 1985; Heller, Sosna, and Wellbery, 1986; Sampson, 1977) have acknowledged individualism's prevalent role in shaping American social institutions and ways of thinking but have criticized it both as destructive of personal development and as undermining societal functioning.

In a similar vein, the idealization of collectivism in the non-Western discourse has not gone unquestioned. Whereas many critics of individualism (for instance, Bellah and others, 1985; Sampson, 1977; Shweder and Bourne, 1982) have idealized collectivism, non-Western scholars have nevertheless expressed criticism about certain aspects of the collectivistic "ethos," such as the unfairness intrinsic to rigid hierarchical systems (Lebra, 1984), the suppression of individual development (Ho and Chiu, 1994), and the limited opportunities for members of disenfranchised groups (Lebra, 1984; Mines, 1988).

The criticisms expressed from within the individualist and collectivist discourse suggest that the unidimensional constructs of individualism and collectivism do not adequately represent the "cultural ethos" of cultures. As discussed above, certain aspects of individualism are criticized in the individualist discourse (for example, the alienation and fragmentation of modern society), and certain aspects of collectivism are rejected in the collectivist discourse (for example, the rigid hierarchies that are typically imposed in traditional cultures). To make things more complex, certain aspects of collectivism (such as family values) and of individualism (such as autonomy) are valued as part of the individualistic and collectivistic cultures respectively. Clearly, the homogeneous templates of individualism and collectivism do not tap the multitude of values and orientations that are part of the public discourse of diverse societies.

Furthermore, we wish to propose that even if certain ideologies were found to be homogeneous enough to be tapped by individualistic or collectivistic discourse, one may not automatically conclude that the *psychological reality* of individuals living in such cultures would actually mirror such an ideology. Indeed, the idea that cultural ideologies are unproblematically reproduced through processes of socialization has been repeatedly challenged (Spiro, 1993; Turiel, 1998; Wainryb and Turiel, 1995). As Strauss (1992, p. 2) aptly put it, "The social order is not a master programmer in any simple, straightforward way." Consequently, analyses of the relation between culture and social development need to account not only for the diversity in cultural symbols, values, and practices, but also for the possibility that individuals in a culture may interpret such symbols, values, and practices in different ways.

Examples of how members of so-called individualistic cultures pursue collectivistic goals and how members of so-called collectivistic cultures pursue individualistic goals abound in the psychological and anthropological literatures. A number of scholars have shown that, in spite of the stated cultural ideology that devalues personal autonomy and goals in favor of adherence to tradition and pursuit of collective goals, persons in traditional cultures value and actively (though often covertly) pursue their own goals and agendas (Spiro, 1993). As an illustration, Mines (1988) examined the life histories of men and women from all strata of Indian society (a reportedly collectivistic, hierarchical society) and documented the ways in which individuals develop personal goals separate from (and often in conflict with) the goals of their social group and take responsibility for the direction of their own lives. Mines found that individuals described themselves as having had personal goals (such as occupational interests or economic goals), and many described such goals as being in clear opposition to societal expectations. However, not all individuals were successful in achieving their life goals, and most postponed pursuing their goals until later in life, when the consequences of such behavior were less extreme (when, for example, disinheritance was no longer a threat). Mines concluded that conformity to traditional expectations is often due to the negative societal consequences of not abiding by such expectations and that it should not be taken—in and of itself—as a sign of a lack of personal goals.

Self-oriented goals, in the form of self-esteem, pride, and power, have also been reported to be part of the lives of villagers in traditional Japanese farming communities (Spiro, 1993) and part of traditional Muslim Arab societies (Abu-Lughod, 1993; Mernissi, 1994). Further evidence for individuals' attempts to realize their personal goals in the context of society's demands for conformity can be seen in the more or less covert processes of maneuvering and negotiation typical of persons in subordinate positions; examples are the behaviors of South Asian women (Ewing, 1990, 1991) and of women in harems (Mernissi, 1994) and polygynous Bedouin societies (Abu-Lughod, 1993).

As a result of the concerns with the mislabeling of cultures and individuals, recognition is emerging that cultures and individuals cannot be accurately described in terms of single categories such as individualism or collectivism and, furthermore, that concerns with issues of independence and interdependence are not mutually exclusive but, rather, are part of the lives of individuals in Western and non-Western cultures (Greenfield and Cocking, 1994; Rosenberger, 1992; Raeff, 1997; Sinha and Tripathi, 1994; Turiel and Wainryb, 1994; Wainryb, 1997).

There are several ways to reconceptualize the categories of individualism and collectivism to explain the coexistence of both types of concerns in a single culture. One way is to view individualism and collectivism not as a dichotomy, but as two ideal types or idealized cultural scripts at opposite poles of a continuum (Greenfield and Cocking, 1994). Within this framework, each society is said to strike a specific balance on the continuum between the two ideal types, which in turn translates into different *proportions* of individualistic and collectivistic elements. Such a position has been espoused by Sinha and Tripathi (1994), who referred to India's exposure to diverse cultural influences through invasions as being responsible for the coexistence (in India) of both individualistic and collectivistic orientations. A similar view underlies explanations of the coexistence of diverse orientations in the United States (Greenfield and Cocking, 1994).

The reconceptualization of individualism and collectivism as a continuum allows for the coexistence of a mixture of concerns; at the same time, such a proposition inevitably raises the question of how these proportions are measured and where on the continuum any given culture is located. In essence, however, the notion implicit in this approach—that of a number of homogeneous (individualistic or collectivistic) subcultures coexisting in a culture—is not significantly different from the approach it is meant to replace—that of a dichotomy between individualistic and collectivistic orientations (Killen, 1997; Wainryb, 1997). An alternative way to account for this coexistence is to locate the source of heterogeneity not at the level of the society but at the level of the individual.

## Coexistence of Social Orientations Within Individuals

By demonstrating that members of diverse cultures value both independence and interdependence, a number of researchers have recently alluded to the proposition that heterogeneity exists at the level of the individual (Nucci and Lee, 1993; Turiel, Killen, and Helwig, 1987; Smetana, 1995; Wainryb and Turiel, 1995). However, identifying the individual as the locus of the mixed orientations raises the question of where such complexity may come from. In our view, the coexistence of individualistic and collectivistic orientations in cultures results from the coexistence of diverse concerns in the lives and the reasoning of individuals. Our position is that, in most cultures, individuals observe and participate in a variety of social interactions that entail experiences with matters as diverse as conflicts over harm and injustice, the enactment of social roles and duties, and opportunities for personal expression and the pursuit of personal entitlements. In the process of participating in and making sense of such multifaceted social experiences, individuals develop distinct types of understandings of, and orientations toward, their social world. These orientations reflect both individualistic (independent) and collectivistic (interdependent) perspectives.

Extensive research carried out in the United States has demonstrated that children begin to form such distinct social orientations at an early age. Young children, for example, recognize that people have personal goals and entitlements that are legitimate in their own right, and they develop concepts about the self and about issues under the jurisdiction of the individual—concepts usually classified as individualistic. At the same time, young children develop concepts about the moral expectations that are part of interpersonal relations. Such moral concepts bear on the collective inasmuch as they refer to concerns with the welfare of others, and they bear on the individual because they pertain to personal rights and entitlements. Children also develop interdependent concerns with roles, authority, and conventions. When taken together, the evidence of over eighty-five studies indicates that, as a result of their interactions with diverse aspects of their social environments, children (as well as adults) simultaneously hold multiple, and often conflicting, concerns with independence and interdependence (for reviews, see Smetana, 1995; Tisak, 1995).

An additional source of heterogeneity in social orientations is the wealth of informational diversity bearing on social and moral decisions. Research has shown that in the process of evaluating social practices, individuals bring to bear not only moral concepts (that is, prescriptions about right and wrong) but also informational beliefs about relevant aspects of reality (that is, beliefs about what is true). Such informational beliefs have been shown to affect the interpretation of social practices and, ultimately, their evaluation (Turiel, Hildebrandt, and Wainryb, 1991; Wainryb, 1991, 1993). Because the application of moral concepts is mediated by beliefs of an informational nature, it is likely that the manifestation of concerns with independence in concrete social situations might yield interdependent decisions, whereas the application of concerns with interdependence may result in the support of independent decisions. It is in this sense that beliefs of an informational nature constitute an additional source of mixture of social orientations.

We wish to highlight that the source of both the coexistence of concerns with independence and interdependence and the varied manifestation of these concerns in concrete social contexts can be located at the level of an active individual interpreting the social world. In our view, the diverse orientations to social judgments and practices reflect distinct, systematic, and organized ways of thinking about the social world and constitute a significant part of social life in cultures.

## The Acquisition of Multiple Social Orientations

Our view regarding the coexistence of different orientations in individuals and in cultures is intrinsically related to our conceptualization of the processes by which such diverse orientations are acquired. I-C theorists (Markus and Kitayama, 1991; Triandis, 1995) have commonly explained the acquisition of individualistic templates in terms of socialization (explicitly teaching values) and the acquisition of collectivistic templates in terms of enculturation (indirectly communicating messages that are absorbed through a process of "osmosis"). In other words, it is commonly thought that children are *either* explicitly taught social values *or* absorb social values; the preferred technique is thought to be a function of culture. Adults in Western cultures are thought to prefer socialization, whereas adults in non-Western cultures are said to prefer enculturation.

Implicit in this acquisition theory are several assumptions that require further examination. First, it is assumed that children are passive recipients of cultural norms and values. Furthermore, it is assumed that adults use a single method of communication to convey values to children. Research conducted over the last several decades, however, has demonstrated that children actively construct social knowledge based on inferences made about their social experiences (Turiel, 1998). Moreover, the acquisition and internalization of social values have been shown to constitute an interactive, not a unilateral, process (Grusec and Goodnow, 1994). Even young children have been shown to evaluate adult messages critically (Grusec and Goodnow, 1994; Killen, Breton, Ferguson, and Handler, 1994; Killen and Nucci, 1995; Nucci and Weber, 1995). In addition, research has shown that adults in diverse cultures use a multitude of techniques—direct and indirect—to communicate values to children. As reported by Grusec and Goodnow (1994), parents use direct teaching in some contexts and indirect teaching in others. Teachers have also been shown to use indirect teaching strategies (for instance, suggestions, alternative choices, and negotiations) regarding issues revolving around autonomy and personal choice (such as dress or choice of friends) and direct teaching strategies (such as explanations or rule statements) regarding moral and social-conventional rules (Killen and Smetana, 1999). This mixture of communication styles, shown to exist in parent-child interaction in both Western and non-Western cultures (in Brazil, Japan, and the United States, for example; Killen and Nucci, 1995), indicates that direct as well as indirect methods of teaching are valued and pursued in both Western and non-Western cultures.

The findings reviewed above do not point to the incorporation of unitary sets of rules, values, or social communications. Instead, the mixture of social orientations in the individual's thinking appears to be consistent with an alternative view of development that posits organized and systematic changes in domains of social reasoning stemming from the individual's varied social interactions and interpretations of different types of social contexts and communications. In the following sections we illustrate aspects of these propositions by drawing on data from our research programs in different societies.

## Independence and Interdependence in Japanese and Colombian School Settings

To examine the proposition of coexistence of social orientations settings outside the United States, studies were conducted in a Japanese preschool in a suburb of Tokyo (Killen and Sueyoshi, 1995) and in several schools in Cartagena, Colombia (Ardila-Rey and Killen, in press). In general, characterizations of Japanese social development have emphasized the collectivistic, interdependent orientations fostered by teachers (Killen and Nucci, 1995). As an illustration, Tobin, Wu, and Davidson (1989), in their ethnographic analysis of preschool life in Japan, China, and the United States, reported that Japanese preschool teachers promote groupism (fostered through the use of uniforms, group activities, and a deemphasis on individual achievements), in contrast to American teachers, who promote self-reliance and independence. An implication of their analysis is that Western teachers deemphasize group conformity and non-Western teachers deemphasize fairness and rights. However, research has raised doubts regarding this characterization. Hamilton, Blumenfeld, Akoh, and Miura (1989) demonstrated that Japanese elementary school teachers use explanations and rationales to a greater extent than their American counterparts, who use more discipline and punishment. Lewis (1995) has observed that Japanese preschool teachers foster self-reliance (independence) through a diminished use of their authority. Further, a survey study with teachers in four countries indicated that teachers in Taiwan, El Salvador, Colombia, and the United States favored explanations and rationales over the use of punishment (Killen, Ardila-Rey, Barakkatz, and Wang, 2000).

In our Japanese study, middle-class preschool-age children ($N = 48$) from a day-care center (a *hoikuen*) in a suburb of Tokyo were observed and interviewed regarding methods of conflict resolution. We found that Japanese children had many conflicts about how to play games (structuring activities) and about how to ensure fairness (distributing resources and taking turns); few conflicts stemmed from physical or psychological harm. These findings revealed that although harmonious relationships may be stressed by "collectivistic" cultures, Japanese children engaged in conflicts. Interestingly, in the Japanese setting, half of the conflicts (51 percent) were resolved by children using compromise and negotiation. Teachers intervened a small percentage (18 percent) of the time, and children used very little retribution (5 percent of the time). When teachers intervened, they used explanations (89 percent of the time) and very few commands and rule statements (11 percent of the time). (By contrast, in American preschool settings, commands and rule statements are the strategy teachers use most frequently; see Smetana, 1984.) Thus, Japanese children had conflicts over issues of rights and fairness (autonomy) and over group cohesiveness (interdependence). Further, teachers used verbal explanations (individualism) *and* feeling statements (collectivism). They refrained from intervening in children's conflicts, thereby *diminishing* their own role as authority figures (this counters the view that harmonious relationships are paramount because otherwise conflicts would be allowed to occur). Finally, evaluations of teacher methods of resolution by children and mothers revealed a mixture of independent and interdependent orientations: in some cases autonomy was stressed, and in others the group was stressed.

From an individualistic versus collectivistic perspective, it might be expected that Japanese children would not have disputes involving issues of fairness or rights, that the group would be more important than the individual, and that children would be passive and obedient to authority (Triandis, 1995). However, issues about rights, fairness, and others' welfare generated conflicts among Japanese preschool-age children; these issues were not found to be specific to Western social interactions. Furthermore, teachers used methods of conflict resolution that emphasized explanations and rationales, which calls into question the view that such methods are the sole prerogative of Western-oriented educators.

Latin American countries have also been classified as "collectivistic" and have been referred to as oriented toward others, or "allocentric" (Marin and Triandis, 1985), to distinguish their collectivism from Asian collectivism. These studies characterize social interactions of Latin Americans as ones of subordination, hierarchy, and acceptance of discipline and punishment. In our study (Ardila-Rey and Killen, in press), children at ages three, five, and seven years ($N = 63$) in middle-class Colombian classrooms were interviewed regarding their evaluation of moral, social-conventional, and personal conflicts. Analyses revealed that, with age, Colombian children preferred teachers to use negotiation and explanation; further, with age, there was a decrease in the preference for teachers to use punishment. Moreover, similar to children in the United States, Colombian children made qualitative distinctions in their evaluation of moral, social-conventional, and personal conflicts.

We believe that independence and interdependence are intertwined in Japanese and Colombian teaching styles, social interactions, and social judgments and that they are not simply present in separate, dichotomous forms. In the Japanese study, the strategy for achieving independence was related to the strategy for encouraging interdependence; the same technique was used to achieve two social goals (teachers diminishing authority to increase self-reliance). In the Colombian study, children valued autonomy and personal choice (independence) as well as cooperative modes of interaction (interdependence). We recognize that the form of independence demonstrated in these interactions may be different from the form used to describe social exchanges in the United States. We do not argue that there are *no* cultural differences in how independence and interdependence are intertwined in diverse cultures. Rather we assert that independence and interdependence coexist in different cultures; the forms of coexistence may vary by teacher and by culture.

## Independence and Interdependence in the Hierarchically Organized Druze Community

An additional illustration of coexisting orientations in individuals and cultures comes from research conducted in the Druze community in Israel (Turiel and Wainryb, 1998; Wainryb, 1995; Wainryb and Turiel, 1994). The Druze live in segregated villages and maintain a social and cultural life that is independent from that of the broader Israeli culture. Their family structure is patrilineal and patriarchal, with rigid distinctions made between males and females. The main features of Druze society are those typically associated with collectivism, which makes this society particularly interesting for examining the interplay of independence and interdependence.

Overall, our research indicated that even though Druze society differs in important ways from Western societies, people in this traditional society form collectivistic judgments about role relations, obedience to authority, and interpersonal obligations and individualistic judgments about persons as autonomous agents with choices and entitlements. At the same time, we learned that concerns with obedience, role relations, and interpersonal obligations were often bounded by individualistic concerns and that issues of personal choice and entitlements were embedded in the hierarchical system. When concerns about interdependence came into conflict with concerns about independence—as they often do—both types of concerns were weighed and coordinated.

One example of the interplay of interdependence and independence can be seen in the Druze conceptions of authority and obedience. Our research with eight- through seventeen-year-olds (Wainryb, 1995) revealed not only the expected collectivistic judgments, but also judgments of a more individualistic nature. As an example, even the youngest children did not uncritically accept the commands of authority figures but, rather, evaluated the legitimacy of such commands and set boundaries to the legitimacy of persons in positions of authority.

Our research also demonstrated that obedience to authority cannot be automatically construed as an acceptance of the cultural hierarchical arrangements. For example, in another study (Wainryb and Turiel, 1994), female adolescents and adults were interviewed about conflict situations in which a person in a dominant position (husband, father) objects to the personal activities of a family member in a subordinate position (wife, daughter), and vice versa. Whereas the majority accepted the legitimacy of males' power and judged that it would be wrong for the person in the subordinate position to disobey, they also judged it acceptable for males to make their own decisions and to disregard females' demands. Noteworthy is the fact that the judgments by females in this society affirming the legitimacy of male authority were grounded on concerns with the negative consequences of disobedience; girls and women believed that husbands and fathers have power to inflict serious harm on them. Furthermore, they also judged that it was unfair for males to dictate females' choices. We concluded that even the prevalence of collectivistic concerns (such as the overriding concern with authority and obedience) does not necessarily reflect a unilateral acceptance of the cultural ideology. Instead, persons in subordinate positions who manifest a concern with obedience do so while cognizant of the potential consequences of failure to acquiesce and while making judgments about the unfairness of such arrangements.

Altogether, this research indicated that individuals in hierarchically organized cultures, such as Druze society, display collectivistic concerns with obedience to authority and, in some contexts, allow such concerns to override personal concerns far more than would be characteristic of individuals in Western cultures. Nevertheless, their thinking about authority, the boundaries they draw on the legitimacy of authority figures, and the complex justifications for acquiescing to the commands of authority figures reveal that their concepts of obedience yield both "collectivistic" decisions (as in the marked legitimacy accorded to male authority) and "individualistic" decisions (as in the boundaries placed on authority figures or in the judgments made about the hierarchical arrangements).

In addition to showing how individuals in traditional societies maintain collectivistic concerns (with the ensuing mixture of social judgments), our research has shown that they also maintain individualistic concepts of persons as autonomous agents and that they judge a range of issues as being within the individual's personal jurisdiction. For example, findings from another study conducted with Druze males (Wainryb and Turiel, 1994) affirmed the common view that interactions in the family involve a strong sense of duties and role prescriptions but also indicated that those interactions include a strong sense of independence. In this study judgments were elicited from adolescent and adult males in reaction to conflict situations between persons in dominant and subordinate positions in the family. The results showed that concepts of persons as autonomous are part of the orientation of males in this hierarchical society. It is also true that alongside such concepts of personal autonomy and entitlements, the males maintained concepts of interdependence. However, the expectations of independence and interdependence between persons were not reciprocal—most participants thought that males should make decisions for themselves as well as for their wives and daughters. It appears that (at least for certain types of interactions in the family) males are conceptualized as autonomous and as legitimately making personal choices. Males are accorded entitlements due to them mostly by those in subordinate positions; women are regarded as dependent on their roles and duties in the system.

In sum, these findings illustrated how concerns with autonomy are not absent from traditional societies but are played out differently for individuals in different roles and positions, resulting in a complex interweaving of independence and interdependence. Furthermore, the perspectives and judgments of those in subordinate positions reflect the struggles and conflicts characteristic of the interplay between opposing orientations in cultures. This is especially noteworthy given that collectivistic societies are presumed to be characterized by coherence and harmony.

What happens in situations of conflict between interdependence and independence? The findings of the two studies examining conflicts in the family (Wainryb and Turiel, 1994) indicated that the Druze subordinate considerations of personal autonomy to the demands of persons in dominant positions more often than would be expected from Western individuals. Nevertheless, the findings of another study (Wainryb, 1995), in which collectivistic goals were placed in conflict with goals considered individualistic, indicated that their preferential orientation toward obedience to authority and interpersonal considerations was not overriding across all contexts and that, in certain cases, the Druze do assert their personal jurisdiction (for example, obedience did not take precedence over matters of justice; concerns with personal choice were often given priority over interpersonal considerations). Finally, in a different study (Turiel and Wainryb, 1998) it was shown that Druze adolescents and adults endorsed freedoms of speech, religion, and reproduction as rights independent of existing laws. When presented with conflict situations in which the freedoms were set against other social considerations of importance to the culture (for example, when the exercise of those freedoms resulted in harm to others or in negative consequences for the community, or when they were in conflict with the directives of an authority figure), they thought that freedoms should be subordinated to the other concerns in *some*—not all—contexts. For example, the majority thought that the freedoms of speech, religion, and reproduction should not be exercised when they result in harmful consequences to others. Similarly, concerns with the community's interest were given precedence over freedoms of speech and reproduction (but not over freedom of religion), and freedom of speech (especially females' freedom) was readily subsumed under the authority of fathers and husbands. By contrast, freedoms of religion and reproduction were generally not subordinated to the authority of fathers or husbands.

Taken together, these findings indicated that the coordination of multiple coexisting concerns in cultures is not done simply according to a unitary cultural orientation. The Druze did not subordinate all concerns with freedoms and personal autonomy to the goals of the collective. Instead, they weighed conflicting concerns while attending to the particular features of the conflict situations. The coordination of conflicting concerns constitutes an additional source of mixture of orientations in cultures.

## Conclusions

In this chapter, we have provided evidence in support of our proposition that cultures and individuals in cultures cannot be accurately described in terms of single categories or orientations, such as individualism and collectivism, or independence and interdependence. This proposition is consistent with the view of an increasing number of researchers and social scientists who have expressed concern that the application of such broad, general categories can result in the stereotyping and mislabeling of cultures. Among those studying the interplay of culture and social development, a consensus has begun to emerge that concern for independence and concern for interdependence, or for the individual and for the group, are not mutually exclusive but, rather, part of the lives and social orientations of members of diverse Western and non-Western cultures alike. "Coexistence of orientations" may be the new, emerging motto.

One interpretation of the coexistence proposition has been that cultures include different proportions of individualistic and collectivistic elements, so that societies can be characterized as being somewhere on the continuum between the poles of individualism and collectivism or independence and interdependence. As we have made clear throughout this chapter, we too believe that cultures (and more specifically, Western and non-Western cultures or cultures that are more or less hierarchically organized) differ in significant ways from each other. In particular (although not exclusively), they differ with regard to the types of social arrangements and the types of social environments they provide to their members as contexts in which social interactions take place. Nevertheless, in our view, the attempt to identify or quantify the *different proportions* of individualistic and collectivistic elements may obscure the complex web of orientations, and their harmonious or conflictive manifestation, that characterize the interactions, behaviors, and reasoning of individuals in cultures.

In this chapter, we have attempted to delineate what, in our view, is a different version of the coexistence proposition. Our data indicate that the locus and source of the divergent, conflicting, and coexisting social orientations in cultures lie at the level of the individual. In the process of participating in and reflecting on multiple types of social interactions, the individual constructs different types of understandings of and orientations toward the social world. The manifestation of these varied orientations in a particular culture's social arrangements, as well as the coordinating of these orientations in conflict situations, results in further mixture and heterogeneity. The conceptual and methodological framework implied in this version of coexistence allows for differentiation among the various components of social development and social reasoning and, in this way, accounts for the complexity of individuals' social thinking and social experiences in and between cultures.

## Note

1. In this field, "individualism" is often equated with "independence," and "collectivism" is often used interchangeably with "interdependence." We define "individualism" and "collectivism" as broad constructs that reflect a wide range of cultural features (social, historical, and economic), and we reserve the terms "independence" and "interdependence" for referring specifically to aspects of social orientations.

## References

Abu-Lughod, L. *Writing Women's Worlds: Bedouin Stories*. Berkeley: University of California Press, 1993.

Ardila-Rey, A., and Killen, M. "Colombian Preschool Children's Judgments About Autonomy and Conflict Resolution in the Classroom Setting." *International Journal of Behavioral Development*, in press.

Bellah, R., and others. *Habits of the Heart*. New York: HarperCollins, 1985.

Berry, J. W. "Ecology and Individualism." In U. Kim, H. C. Triandis, Ç. Kagitçibasi, S. Choi, and G. Yoon (eds.), *Individualism and Collectivism: Theory, Method, and Applications*. San Anselmo, Calif.: Sage Press, 1994.

Ewing, K. "The Illusion of Wholeness: Culture, Self and the Experience of Inconsistency." *Ethos*, 1990, *18*, 251–278.

Ewing, K. "Can Psychoanalytic Theories Explain the Pakistani Woman? Intrapsychic Autonomy and Interpersonal Engagement in the Extended Family." *Ethos*, 1991, *19*, 131–160.

Fromm, E. *Escape from Freedom*. Austin, Tex.: Holt, Rinehart and Winston, 1941.

Geertz, C. "Life on the Edge." *New York Review of Books*, 1994, 3–4.

Greenfield, P. M., and Cocking, R. R. (eds.). *Cross-Cultural Roots of Minority Child Development*. Mahwah, N.J.: Erlbaum, 1994.

Grusec, J., and Goodnow, J. "Impact of Parental Discipline Methods on the Child's Internalization of Values: A Reconceptualization of Current Points of View." *Developmental Psychology*, 1994, *30*, 4–19.

Hamilton, V. L., Blumenfeld, P., Akoh, H., and Miura, K. "Citizenship and Scholarship in Japanese and American Fifth Grades." *American Educational Research Journal*, 1989, *26*, 44–72.

Heller, T., Sosna, M., and Wellbery, D. *Reconstructing Individualism*. Stanford, Calif.: Stanford University Press, 1986.

Ho, D.Y.F., and Chiu, C.-Y. "Component Ideas of Individualism, Collectivism and Social Organization: An Application in the Study of Chinese Culture." In U. Kim, H. C. Triandis, Ç. Kagitçibasi, S. Choi, and G. Yoon (eds.), *Individualism and Collectivism: Theory, Method, and Applications*. San Anselmo, Calif.: Sage Press, 1994.

Hofstede, G. *Culture's Consequences: International Differences in Work-Related Values.* San Anselmo, Calif.: Sage Press, 1980.

Hsu, F.L.K. *Rugged Individualism Reconsidered.* Knoxville: University of Tennessee Press, 1983.

Kagitçibasi, Ç., and Berry, J. W. "Cross-Cultural Psychology: Current Research and Trends." *Annual Review of Psychology,* 1989, *40,* 493–531.

Killen, M. "Culture, Self, and Development: Are Cultural Templates Useful or Stereotypic?" *Developmental Review,* 1997, *17,* 239–249.

Killen, M., Ardila-Rey, A., Barakkatz, M., and Wang, P. "Preschool Teachers' Perceptions About Conflict Resolution, Autonomy, and the Group in Four Countries: United States, Colombia, El Salvador, and Taiwan." *Early Education and Development,* 2000, *11,* 73–92.

Killen, M., Breton, S., Ferguson, H., and Handler, K. "Preschoolers' Evaluations of Teacher Methods of Intervention in Social Transgressions." *Merrill-Palmer Quarterly,* 1994, *40,* 399–416.

Killen, M., and Nucci, L. P. "Morality, Autonomy, and Social Conflict." In M. Killen and D. Hart (eds.), *Morality in Everyday Life: Developmental Perspectives.* New York: Cambridge University Press, 1995.

Killen, M., and Smetana, J. G. "Social Interactions in Preschool Classrooms and the Development of Young Children's Conceptions of the Personal." *Child Development,* 1999, *70,* 486–501.

Killen, M., and Sueyoshi, L. "Conflict Resolution in Japanese Preschool Interactions." *Early Education and Development,* 1995, *6,* 313–330.

Kim, U., Triandis, H. C., Kagitçibasi, Ç., Choi, S., and Yoon, G. (eds.). *Individualism and Collectivism: Theory, Method, and Applications.* San Anselmo, Calif.: Sage Press, 1994.

Lebra, T. S. *Japanese Women: Constraint and Fulfillment.* Honolulu: University of Hawaii Press, 1984.

Lewis, C. C. *Educating Hearts and Minds: Reflections on Japanese Preschool and Elementary Education.* New York: Cambridge University Press, 1995.

Marin, G., and Triandis, H. C. "Allocentrism as an Important Characteristic of the Behaviors of Latin Americans and Hispanics." In R. Diaz-Guerrero (ed.), *Cross-Cultural and National Studies in Social Psychology.* Amsterdam: Elsevier, 1985.

Markus, H. R., and Kitayama, S. "Culture and the Self: Implications for Cognition, Emotion, and Motivation." *Psychological Review,* 1991, *98,* 224–253.

Mednick, M. "On the Politics of Psychological Constructs: Stop the Bandwagon, I Want to Get Off." *American Psychologist,* 1989, *44,* 1118–1123.

Mernissi, F. *Dreams of Trespass: Tales of a Harem Girlhood.* Reading, Mass.: Addison-Wesley, 1994.

Mills, C. W. *White Collar: The American Middle Class.* New York: Oxford University Press, 1956.

Mines, M. "Conceptualizing the Person: Hierarchical Society and Individual Autonomy in India." *American Anthropologist,* 1988, *90,* 568–579.

Nucci, L. P., and Lee, J. "Morality and Personal Autonomy." In G. G. Noam and T. Wren (eds.), *The Moral Self: Building a Better Paradigm.* Cambridge, Mass.: MIT Press, 1993.

Nucci, L. P., and Weber, E. "Social Interactions in the Home and the Development of Young Children's Conceptions of the Personal." *Child Development,* 1995, *66,* 1438–1452.

Overton, W. "Developmental Psychology: Philosophy, Concepts, and Methodology." In W. Damon (series ed.), *Handbook of Child Psychology* (5th ed), Vol. 1: *Theoretical Models of Human Development* (R. Lerner, volume ed.). New York: Wiley, 1998, 107–188.

Raeff, C. "Individuals in Relationships: Cultural Values, Children's Social Interactions, and the Development of an American Individualistic Self." *Developmental Review,* 1997, 17.

Reisman, D., Glazer, N., and Denney, R. *The Lonely Crowd: A Study of the Changing American Character.* New York: Doubleday, 1953.

Rosenberger, N. *Japanese Sense of Self*. New York: Cambridge University Press, 1992.

Sampson, E. "Psychology and the American Ideal." *Journal of Personality and Social Psychology*, 1977, *35*, 767–782.

Shweder, R. A., and Bourne, E. J. "Does the Concept of Person Vary Cross-Culturally?" In A. J. Marsella and G. M. White (eds.), *Cultural Conceptions of Mental Health and Therapy*. Boston: Reidel, 1982.

Sinha, D., and Tripathi, R. "Individualism in a Collectivistic Culture: A Case of Coexistence of Opposites." In U. Kim, H. C. Triandis, Ç. Kagitçibasi, S. Choi, and G. Yoon (eds.), *Individualism and Collectivism: Theory, Method, and Applications*. San Anselmo, Calif.: Sage Press, 1994.

Smetana, J. G. "Toddlers' Social Interactions Regarding Moral and Conventional Transgressions." *Child Development*, 1984, *55*, 1767–1776.

Smetana, J. G. "Morality in Context: Abstractions, Ambiguities, and Applications." *Annals of Child Development*, 1995, *10*, 83–130.

Spiro, M. "Is the Western Conception of the Self 'Peculiar' Within the Context of the World Cultures?" *Ethos*, 1993, *21*, 107–153.

Strauss, C. "Models and Motives." In R. D'Andrade and C. Strauss (eds.), *Human Motives and Cultural Models*. New York: Cambridge University Press, 1992.

Tisak, M. "Domains of Social Reasoning and Beyond." *Annals of Child Development*, 1995, *11*, 95–130.

Tobin, J. J., Wu, D.Y.H., and Davidson, D. H. *Preschool in Three Cultures: Japan, China, and the United States*. New Haven, Conn.: Yale University Press, 1989.

Triandis, H. C. *Individualism and Collectivism*. Boulder, Colo.: Westview Press, 1995.

Turiel, E. "Morality, Authoritarianism, and Personal Agency." In R. J. Sternberg and P. Ruzgis (eds.), *Personality and Intelligence*. New York: Cambridge University Press, 1994.

Turiel, E. "The Development of Morality." In W. Damon (series ed.), *Handbook of Child Psychology* (5th ed.), Vol. 3: *Social, Emotional, and Personality Development* (N. Eisenberg, volume ed.). New York: Wiley, 1998.

Turiel, E., Hildebrandt, C., and Wainryb, C. "Judging Social Issues: Difficulties, Inconsistencies, and Consistencies." *Monographs of the Society for Research in Child Development*, 1991, *56*(224).

Turiel, E., Killen, M., and Helwig, C. "Morality: Its Structure, Functions, and Vagaries." In J. Kagan and S. Lamb (eds.), *The Emergence of Morality in Young Children*. Chicago: University of Chicago Press, 1987.

Turiel, E., and Wainryb, C. "Social Reasoning and the Varieties of Social Experience in Cultural Contexts." In H. W. Reese (ed.), *Advances in Child Development and Behavior*. Vol. 25. Orlando, Fla.: Academic Press, 1994.

Turiel, E., and Wainryb, C. "Concepts of Freedoms and Rights in a Traditional, Hierarchically Organized Society." *British Journal of Developmental Psychology*, 1998, *16*, 375–395.

Wainryb, C. "Understanding Differences in Moral Judgments: The Role of Informational Assumptions." *Child Development*, 1991, *62*, 840–851.

Wainryb, C. "The Application of Moral Judgments to Other Cultures: Relativism and Universality." *Child Development*, 1993, *64*, 924–933.

Wainryb, C. "Reasoning About Social Conflicts in Different Cultures: Druze and Jewish Children in Israel." *Child Development*, 1995, *66*, 390–401.

Wainryb, C. "The Mismeasure of Diversity: Reflections on the Study of Cross-Cultural Differences." In H. D. Saltzstein (ed.), *Culture as a Context for Moral Development: New Perspectives on the Particular and the Universal*. New Directions for Child Development, no. 76, 51–65. San Francisco: Jossey-Bass, 1997.

Wainryb, C., and Turiel, E. "Dominance, Subordination, and Concepts of Personal Entitlements in Cultural Contexts." *Child Development*, 1994, *65*, 1701–1722.

Wainryb, C., and Turiel, E. "Diversity in Social Development: Between or Within Cultures?" In M. Killen and D. Hart (eds.), *Morality in Everyday Life: Developmental Perspectives*. New York: Cambridge University Press, 1995.

Whyte, W. H. *The Organization Man*. New York: Simon & Schuster, 1956.

MELANIE KILLEN *is professor of human development and associate director of the Center for Children, Relationships, and Culture at the University of Maryland, College Park.*

CECILIA WAINRYB *is associate professor of psychology at the University of Utah, Salt Lake City.*

# 2

*Research on Dutch and American parents' descriptions
and interpretations of their children's personality and
behavior reveals a systematic pattern of difference that
defies the idea of a uniform "Western mind" characterized
by individualism.*

# Individualism and the "Western Mind" Reconsidered: American and Dutch Parents' Ethnotheories of the Child

*Sara Harkness, Charles M. Super, Nathalie van Tijen*

As studies of thinking among peoples of many cultures have accumulated in recent years, the idea of a distinctive "Western mind" with its own unique conceptualization of the self has gained acceptance among scholars in anthropology, sociology, and psychology. At the core of this conceptualization is the idea of the self as separate from the social environment. As Geertz (1984, p. 126) describes it, "The Western conception of the person as a bounded, unique, more or less integrated motivational and cognitive universe, a dynamic center of awareness, emotion, judgment, and action organized into a distinctive whole and set contrastively both against other such wholes and against its social and natural background is, however incorrigible it may seem to us, a rather peculiar idea within the context of the world's cultures."

The idea of a distinctive "Western mind" as opposed to its non-Western counterpart is very close to the contrasting constructs of individualism or independence versus sociocentrism, collectivism, or interdependence. Each of these constructs can be thought of as a cultural metamodel, a cluster of ideas that characterize cultures at a broad level and that should logically have wide-ranging functions for the organization of human development and

The research reported here was supported by grants from the Spencer Foundation and the National Science Foundation. All statements made and views expressed are the sole responsibility of the authors.

social relationships. The mediating link between these cultural metamodels and behavior is parental ethnotheories—cultural belief systems that parents hold regarding the nature of children, development, parenting, and the family (Harkness and Super, 1996). The findings of cross-cultural research on parents' ideas about children are consistent with this general contrast. For example, Harkness and Super's research (1992) on parents in a rural Kipsigis community of Kenya and a middle-class American sample in the Boston area draws a contrast between concepts of the child that emphasize obedience, responsibility, and socially situated intelligence in the Kipsigis group and independence and school-related cognitive skills in the American group.

Although the concept of an individualistic "Western mind" seems useful for analyzing differences in relation to non-Western peoples, a growing body of research indicates that the cultural boundaries of this construct cannot easily be delineated on a map of the world. For example, immigrant groups in the United States, including those of Latin American origin, have been contrasted to the mainstream American middle class in terms of interdependence versus independence (Greenfield and Cocking, 1994). Research on developmental timetables among Italian and American parents and preschool teachers also indicates that expectations for early development—consistent with an individualistic concept of the self—are not equally shared in these two settings (Edwards, Gandini, and Giovaninni, 1996). A question then arises: Where does the "Western mind" reside?

In this chapter, we challenge the idea of a unitary "Western mind" and reexamine the constructs of individualism and sociocentrism through an analysis of parents' cultural models of the child in two Western, socioeconomically similar populations: one in the United States and the other in the Netherlands. Using parents' descriptions of their own children as evidence for implicit cultural models of "the child," we find patterns of similarity and difference between the two groups that belie both the assumed homogeneity of the "Western mind" and the integrity of individualism and sociocentrism as cross-cultural dimensions of contrast. The ways that parents in both the U.S. and Dutch communities describe and comment on their own children, we find, require a new conceptualization of the individual in social context, which we discuss at the end of the chapter.

Our data come from studies of parents and children in the environs of Cambridge, Massachusetts, in the United States, during the late 1980s and in a town (which we will refer to by the pseudonym "Bloemenheim") near Leiden, in the Netherlands, where we carried out field research in 1992 and subsequently from 1995 to 1996. Cambridge, best known for its major universities and colleges, is home to a diverse population, including many different ethnic groups and social classes. The thirty-six families in the Cambridge study were recruited through a large health maintenance organization located in the city, but most of the participating families lived in surrounding towns. Bloemenheim is a town that lies in the heart of a densely populated area stretching from Amsterdam to The Hague. Although still surrounded by the famous bulb fields,

Bloemenheim has grown from an agricultural community to include light industry as well as new housing for commuters to the nearby cities and towns. Sixty-six families recruited through school and neighborhood networks in Bloemenheim participated in the original 1992 study, which provides the basis for the present analyses.

The sample of American families included target children in three cohorts—newborn, eighteen months old, and thirty-six months old—who were followed longitudinally over the course of a year and a half, until they reached the ages of eighteen months, thirty-six months, and four and one-half years respectively. The Dutch sample included families with children evenly divided into five age cohorts (six months, eighteen months, three years, four and one-half years, and seven to eight years). Both samples were balanced for sex and birth order of the target children (firstborn versus later born). For the present analyses, we draw on data collected from children ages eighteen months, thirty-six months, and four and one-half years in each cultural sample (a total of twenty-nine American families and thirty-four Dutch families). The Cambridge families were almost entirely of European ancestry; the ethnic background of virtually all families in Bloemenheim was northern European, as is typical in all but the major cities of the Netherlands today. Families in both samples were culturally normative, intact, and nuclear, with at least one parent employed and no major health problems. The Dutch and American parents were generally similar in age, and both samples included a range of variability in socioeconomic status, from skilled worker to professional (Hollingshead categories IV to I; see Super and others, 1996), although the Cambridge sample was more heavily weighted toward the upper end of the scale.

## Cultural Models of the Child in Parental Descriptions

A central component of the research was parent interviews, carried out in the home with both parents together; interviews were tape-recorded and later transcribed. Parents' descriptions of their children occurred frequently throughout these interviews in the context of talking about the child's daily routines, current developmental changes, behavioral issues, and parents' goals for the child. In the Bloemenheim interviews, we also asked parents to "describe your child."

Quite early in our interviews with the Bloemenheim parents, it became evident that parents' stories and descriptions of their children were rather different in orientation and emphasis from what we had previously heard from the Cambridge parents. Parents in the Cambridge sample often described their children in terms of their intelligence, which parents attributed to them at the earliest possible age. In talking about their children, these parents typically professed to be "amazed" at their children's abilities, which they found "remarkable" by comparison with other children of the same age or in contrast to what they might have imagined a small child to be capable of. For example, a mother of a three-year-old girl described the behavior of her child as a newborn and related it to her current perceptions of the child:

> I have this vivid memory when she was born of them taking her to clean her off and put the blanket around her and all that. And she was looking all around. She was looking at us. She was looking around the delivery room. She was alert from the very first second. Even when I would take her out— I took her out when she was six weeks old to a shopping mall to have her picture taken—people would stop me and say, "What an alert baby." One guy stopped me and said, "Lady, you have an intelligent baby there." An intelligent child. And it was just something about her. She was very engaging and very with the program, very observant. She's still fabulously observant [Interview 109-1-1].

Likewise, a father described his three-year-old son as "active" not only physically but cognitively:

> Yes, he's a very active child. He needs to be very active. He needs to play with children who are at a certain level of sophistication. You can't sit around the house all day. On weekends we've got to take him to a museum or park or something or he'll be impossible. Now I can see that sort of fits a pattern [Interview 133-1-139].

In both of these descriptions, parents point to their child's superior cognitive abilities, which are manifested in a variety of ways: looking, type of play, need for mental stimulation. The children in these descriptions are active beings who are *using* the environment (whether social or material) to develop their own internally driven need for knowledge and understanding. The parents seem to refer to the child's environment—including even themselves—as existing to serve the needs of the child for optimal individual development.

In contrast to the Cambridge parents, the Bloemenheim parents tended to emphasize the child's social qualities. The parents of a three-year-old girl offered the following response to our request to describe the child:

MOTHER:  Yes, hmm. Very sweet, but also at the stage where she gets angry rather quickly. . . . also very cozy, likes to do everything with you in the house, whatever you're busy with, chatters nicely, also likes to clean the windows. Loves to sing. . . . she really finds everything nice, she likes lots of different things. [*To the father*] Do you know of anything more good or bad?
FATHER:  Yes, she is now in a stage of trying hard to figure out what are the limits. How far can I go before Daddy will get mad? Or before I say, "Hey don't do that!" Or "Now that's enough." And that is trying to push out the boundaries of what is allowed and what isn't. . . . So at this age, and we've seen it also in the older two, there is a certain period when they try to find

out how far they can go. Sometimes it's hard not to get angry about things that they don't yet understand aren't allowed.

MOTHER: She also plays well with other children.

FATHER: Yes. And she is also—not that I think this is a "must"—but she is also very adaptable, and I think that comes from what she sees in her environment. That she can play by herself, or just sit nicely somewhere with one of her parents, or with other children. And that she can also let other children play with her toys.

MOTHER: [*Laughing*] She can also fight nicely with other children [Interview 227-1-139].

In these parents' descriptions of their daughter, the central theme is sociability. The mother first describes her as good company—a child who is pleasant and likes to do everything with her around the house. The father focuses on her development in terms of learning the boundaries of acceptable behavior, a social domain. The mother then describes the girl as socially competent with other children (though adding at the end that "she can also fight nicely"), and the father elaborates on the theme of social competence by describing her as able to play either with others or by herself.

Thus, in these examples the Cambridge parents' descriptions of their children emphasize individualistic qualities; by contrast, the Bloemenheim parents focus on the child as a social being. Whereas the environment in the Cambridge descriptions seems to function primarily as a necessary resource for the child's individual development, in Bloemenheim the central task of development seems to be learning how to function successfully as a member of a social world. On the other hand, a closer look at the Bloemenheim parents' description of their daughter also reveals a concern with cognition (albeit in a social domain—learning the boundaries of what is allowed) and with the ability to entertain oneself and play alone—presumably a mark of independence and maturity.

As we reflected on observations such as these, it struck us that such differences mirror the more general contrast between individualism and sociocentrism, but with some intriguing exceptions. In order to test the validity of this interpretation and explore cultural differences further, we devised two analytic strategies: first, a comparison of the occurrence of relevant descriptors in parental discourse about children; and second, an analysis of how parents in each cultural sample talked about the core constructs of dependence and independence.

## Parents' Descriptions of Their Children: A Quantitative Analysis

The extent to which different kinds of descriptors are used to characterize one's own child, we assume, reflects the degree of importance that parents attach to the qualities mentioned. Such qualities, furthermore, can be mentioned in either a positive framework, in which the child is described as possessing the quality, or in a negative framework, in which the child is described as lacking it. In order to measure the relative importance of different qualities in parents' descriptions of their children, we identified various kinds of descriptors given in the interviews, whether presented in the form of attributes (for example, "He's a very happy boy") or in terms of frequent behavior (for example, "She loves to play on the swings"). The descriptors were coded by both Dutch and American investigators according to judgments of similarity in meaning that preserved local distinctions but made possible comparisons between the two samples, eliminating repetitions in the same speaking turn. The proportion of descriptors in each category was then computed separately for each child, based on all the descriptors the parents used for the child. (This is similar to, but less constrained than, the approach used by Kohnstamm, Halverson, and colleagues in their developmental study of the "big five" dimensions of personality; see Kohnstamm, Halverson, Havill, and Mervielde, 1996.)

For present purposes, we are concerned with descriptors that can be further categorized as either individualistic or sociocentric; together these typically constitute about 60 percent of the descriptors for each child. (The remainder, not discussed here, concern temperament—about 30 percent—or fall into a residual category of "other"—about 7 percent.) Individualistic descriptors include those related to being *smart,* talented or advanced, *interested* in or curious about the surrounding world, *enterprising* or achievement oriented, *self-confident, independent,* a *leader,* and *strong willed.* All these descriptors refer to the individual as distinct from the social environment. The sociocentric category was defined to include only two kinds of descriptors: *sociable* (including being friendly, sharing, liking other people, or liking to be with other people) and *obedient.* Sociability lies at the heart of a sociocentric orientation toward the group, and obedience has been frequently noted as typical of sociocentric cultures. Finally, being *dependent* or seeking attention can be seen either as related to egocentrism, an individualistic quality, or as a manifestation of interdependence, a quality ascribed to sociocentric societies.

Table 2.1 shows the average proportions of use of each descriptor category for the Cambridge and Bloemenheim parents, together with the results of $t$ tests for group differences. As Table 2.1 shows, our impression of greater emphasis on intelligence among the Cambridge parents is confirmed in the significant difference in rates of use for that category. In fact, for the Cambridge parents the *smart* category is by far the largest group of descriptors, comprising almost one-fifth of all descriptors and more than twice the rate of this category for the Bloemenheim parents. The individualistic descriptors *self-confident* and *leader* also are significantly more common among the Cambridge parents, although the overall rates in both samples are much lower.

Our impression of more attention to social qualities on the part of the Bloemenheim parents is also borne out by the corresponding rates for *sociable.* Interestingly, the rates of occurrence of this descriptor and *smart*

**Table 2.1. Sample Differences in Rates of Individualistic and Sociocentric Descriptors of Children**

| Descriptor | Bloemenheim (Percentage) | Cambridge (Percentage) | t (61) | p <= |
|---|---|---|---|---|
| Individualistic | | | | |
| Smart[a] | 9.1 | 19.3 | 4.47 | .000 |
| Interested | 3.9 | 5.1 | 1.07 | n.s. |
| Enterprising[a] | 3.2 | 1.2 | −2.53 | .01 |
| Self-confident[a] | 1.2 | 3.5 | 2.55 | .01 |
| Independent | 4.5 | 4.1 | −0.33 | n.s. |
| Dependent | 4.5 | 4.0 | −0.35 | n.s. |
| Leader | 2.5 | 5.4 | 1.99 | .05 |
| Strong willed | 7.5 | 3.9 | −2.87 | .006 |
| Total | 36.3 | 46.4 | 3.70 | .0005 |
| Sociocentric | | | | |
| Sociable[a] | 17.6 | 12.7 | −2.40 | .02 |
| Obedient[a] | 5.7 | 5.9 | 0.87 | n.s. |
| Total | 23.2 | 18.6 | −1.80 | .08 |
| Overall total | 57 | 60 | | |

Note: n.s. = not significant.
[a]Includes opposites (for example, "not very smart").

are the mirror image of each other in the two samples, with *sociable* being the most frequent descriptor type for the Dutch parents, followed by *smart*, whereas the opposite is true for the American parents. Thus, the proposition that the Bloemenheim and Cambridge parents' ideas about children can be contrasted in terms of the global categories of individualism and sociocentrism receives some support from this measure of descriptor use. There are also several exceptions to the predicted differences in relation to other descriptors, however. Most notably, the descriptors *dependent* and *independent* were equally attributed to children in both samples, as were *obedient* and *interested;* and the qualities of being *strong willed* and *enterprising* were mentioned *more* frequently by the Bloemenheim parents.

We have argued elsewhere (Super and others, 1996) that differences of this sort cannot be reduced to a common variable, such as parental education, and that instead they reflect qualitatively distinct configurations of cultural meaning. Support for this view is found in the near absence of correlations between maternal and paternal education, on the one hand, and the twelve indices (the ten descriptors plus the total of each of the two classes of descriptors) presented in Table 2.1 (tested separately within the sample). Of the forty-eight correlations shown in Table 2.1, only one reaches statistical significance—approximately the level that can be expected by chance, given the close relationship of the two education measures. (The significant correlation occurs in Cambridge, where families with more educated fathers are more likely to describe their children as being *enterprising*: $r = .47$, $p = .001$.) Not surprisingly, therefore, we also found that removing the effect of parental education in the pooled samples and then testing again for group differences did not alter our conclusions. Although this procedure does reduce the strength of the group differences (as any variance common to sample and education is now assigned to the latter), the pattern of differences seen in Table 2.1 remains: the group differences in *smart, enterprising, strong willed, sociable,* and the Individualistic total continue to be statistically significant.

The key to understanding the cultural meanings of these differing patterns of descriptors lies in the context, or how they are used in discourse. We turn, therefore, to a more detailed examination of how parents talked about the core concepts of dependence and independence in their children. The concept of independence is central to individualism, while dependence may be relevant to both individualism and sociocentrism. A closer look at these two constructs in context may help in understanding other aspects of parental descriptions as well.

## Cultural Concepts of Dependence

Both Bloemenheim and Cambridge parents talked about dependence in terms of two main kinds of behavior: (1) seeking attention; (2) seeking comfort, proximity, physical contact, or affection. This operational definition of dependence corresponds closely to the behavioral categories used in a major cross-cultural study of social behavior in children (Whiting and Edwards, 1988) and would seem to be a good candidate for a universally recognizable parental construct. Whereas the Cambridge and Bloemenheim parents agreed on what constitutes dependent behavior, however, they differed considerably in their interpretations of and responses to such behavior.

The Bloemenheim parents whose discourse could be coded ($n = 19$) referred to two main qualities that we include in the category of "dependence": attention seeking (*aandacht-vragend*) and dependence itself (as described by the term *aanhankelijk,* "dependent"). All of the Bloemenheim families in this subsample considered these kinds of behavior basically normal and positive in young children. In fact, when asked what they thought their children most needed for their development right now, parents frequently responded "attention." As the father of an eighteen-month-old boy said:

> He really needs attention, and through that you see him growing. He's learn-
> ing how to talk. . . . it's not just *one* thing. It's a combination of factors. Just
> the attention from us, from his older brother . . . the examples from his
> brother . . . He does things following his brother. And . . . the love that he
> gets. Also from his grandfather and grandmother, and his uncle. . . . that is
> for me at this moment the most important thing. And his little bowl of por-
> ridge every morning [*laughs*] [Interview 202-1-237].

Similarly, the father of a four-year-old boy commented:

> He is a boy who asks for affirmation, he does something and then he comes to ask. You have to give him attention and that's not a problem because it's normal. If he's playing outside then he also gets attention from other children, especially the older children here in the neighborhood. I just think he really needs that. I think that if we didn't give him attention then he would do things that aren't allowed, he would start getting into mischief [Interview 236-1-222].

As expressed here, the Bloemenheim parents suggested that if children demand attention, it is because they need it and that the demand should be satisfied, within the limits of parents' interest and availability.

Children who were very affectionate and needed lots of cuddles were called "dependent" or "snuggle-bunnies" (*knuffeldiertjes*). This quality was accepted as part of the child's innate character:

> FATHER:  She is also very affectionate, I think, she always creeps up to you.
> MOTHER:  Dependent.
> FATHER:  Dependent, yes.
> MOTHER:  She's a snuggle-bunny [Interview 230-1-97].

Parents noticed individual differences in children's demands for attention; but even those children who made it impossible for parents to focus on anything else in the child's presence were not deemed problematic. As the mother of an eighteen-month-old boy recounted:

> If I'm sitting with the newspaper or a book, then it has to be put aside, and then if I pick it up again later he comes here and sits on top of it, so I just think, "Well, I can do that in the evening." But if he's busy playing then I can just go wash the dishes or something like that, but as soon as it's like, "Oh, she's not looking at me anymore," then he needs attention again.

After describing more of such behavior in his son, the father concludes:

> You can really notice that he needs a lot of attention, but it's not troublesome [Interview 239-1-179].

Some parents attributed their child's attention-seeking behavior to experience rather than the child's nature. According to all of them, however, the child's behavior was natural, reasonable, and not a cause for concern. For example, one mother explained that her daughter demanded extra attention because she was used to it, since the mother had been at home with her since birth.

In summary, many Bloemenheim parents described their children as attention-seeking or emotionally dependent, but they did not seem to worry about this. Dependent behavior was understood as normal for young children in general or as a characteristic of the particular child. In a few cases, parents also gave environmental explanations but characterized the child's response as natural and reasonable. Parents themselves enjoyed snuggling or playing with their children but were ready to set limits when they needed to, without feeling guilty. Giving attention and love was seen as one of the most important things parents could do for their children. Parents felt that children's requests for attention and affection should be granted but that children should also learn to play by themselves and not be entirely dependent on others to be entertained.

In contrast to the Bloemenheim parents' generally positive perceptions of dependence in their children, none of the twelve Cambridge couples who talked about dependence described this behavior as normal or desirable. Instead, the attention-seeking child was characterized as "craving" attention or "clingy," and the behavior was described as problematic for the parents. A major issue raised by these parents was the child's difficulty in sharing parental attention with others. The mother of three children, for example, commented about her four-year-old son:

> Somehow it's doing things with all of them that seems difficult, but you can do almost anything with Jonathan by himself. And you can take him anywhere and he'll be generally very accommodating just because he is then the sole focus of attention [Interview 102-4-36].

A particularly dramatic example of the child's need for her mother's undivided attention was recounted by a mother who had spent the day "doing her colors" with a visiting friend:

> Nancy [the friend] and I did it and Marcie [the three-year-old daughter] was just around us. While we'd include her periodically, she was just there and I wasn't making a special effort to do special things with her. Well, by the end of the day, she had a temper tantrum like I have never seen before. John [the husband] was out of town. It went on for at least 45 minutes of screaming and kicking and crying and stuff. I mean I've never seen it—it made me realize that here she had been—here Nancy was taking my attention and Marcie was having a very hard time sharing me. She has had a hard enough time sharing me with Matthew [the younger brother]. Here a friend of mine had been here since Sunday that she had to share me with. By Thursday she had just had it [Interview 108-4-12].

As in the above quote, an idea expressed by several parents was that the child's dependent behavior was the unfortunate consequence of stresses in the environment. In a similar vein, the mother of a four-year-old girl described hassles at the child's preschool and their own busy schedule to her daughter's excessive demands for attention at home and at school:

If a child comes to give me a hug, she's immediately over hugging me—"my mommy, my mommy." That kind of stuff. [What] I have also noticed since we've been both so busy the last few weeks—I think Bob [the father] has noticed it too—is very much more, I wouldn't say clinginess, but constantly coming back for hugs and kisses, wanting to have hugs and kisses, and a lot more than . . . before, and wanting me to sit down and watch *Sesame Street* in the morning, the need to be there. Like tonight, she didn't want me to leave her. She wanted me to be up there and read stories and sing her a lullaby and that kind of stuff, to the point where it drives you crazy [Interview 117-4-17].

Even more distressing for this mother than the child's demanding behavior itself, however, was the thought that perhaps it reflected a problem for which the mother herself might be to blame:

I get upset and it bothers me that she might think that she needs to—it both-ers me that she needs to reach out—this is what I think—that she needs to reach out a little bit more to us. Like right now she's clingier with me. That bothers me because I think, "Well, does that mean that I don't . . ." Not that I don't love her as much, but I'm not spending as much time with her. I really—I've always felt, and they told us this when we went for our refresher course—we went for our refresher course at childbirth classes. The nurse said to us, when I was pregnant with Megan, "You will probably feel guilt with the second one that you just don't spend the time with the second that you did with the first one." So, with that on my mind all the time, I'm always feeling, "Gee, did I spend more time with Amos?" She's not getting as much 'cause now I'm working. Now I'm at the nursery school working. Even though she sees me all morning at the nursery school, still I'm with other children. So I'm constantly feeling that pressure, if you want to call it pressure. It's always there [Interview 117-4-212].

As is evident in these excerpts, some of the Cambridge parents gave the impression that they were rather stressed, in contrast to the typically calm and cheerful Bloemenheim parents. On the other hand, they seemed to demand more of themselves in terms of devoting time exclusively to the child, even though they expressed more impatience with it than did the Bloemenheim parents. It appears that these Cambridge parents found dependent, attention-seeking behavior problematic in a way that the Bloemenheim parents did not.

Table 2.2 summarizes these differences in terms of percentages of parents in each cultural sample who expressed each major theme. As is evident from Table 2.2, parents in Bloemenheim were significantly more likely to discuss dependence as a normal, nonproblematic phenomenon than were the Cambridge parents. The Bloemenheim parents also more frequently (although not significantly) described dependent behavior as an aspect of the child's innate character. Conversely, the Cambridge parents much more

**Table 2.2. Sample Differences in Meaning of "Dependent" Behavior**

| Meaning | Bloemenheim (Percentage) | Cambridge (Percentage) | Chi-Square | p <= |
|---|---|---|---|---|
| Dependence | | | | |
| Normal[a] | 42 | 8 | 4.07 | .04 |
| Innate to child[a] | 63 | 33 | 2.62 | n.s. |
| Problem, needing change[a] | 11 | 75 | 13.35 | .001 |
| Result of experience[a] | 21 | 42 | 1.51 | n.s. |
| Experiential effect | | | | |
| Positive adaptation[b] | 100 | 0 | | .008[c] |
| Stress[b] | 0 | 100 | | .008[c] |

Note: n.s. = not significant.

[a]n = 19 for Bloemenheim, n = 12 for Cambridge.

[b]n = 4 for Bloemenheim, n = 5 for Cambridge.

[c]p of Fisher's exact test.

frequently viewed dependent behavior as a problem requiring change, and they also mentioned experiential causes somewhat more frequently. Of those parents who mentioned environmental causes in each sample, it is striking that the Cambridge parents mentioned only negative experience, whereas Bloemenheim parents mentioned only positive experience. Thus, even though the two sets of parents identified similar child behaviors as dependent, they were working with different understandings of the causes, significance, and implications of such behavior.

## The Significance of Independence

Like dependence, the concept of independence also encompasses a variety of behaviors that parents in both settings recognized as expressions of independence, but with significant differences in meaning (summarized in Table 2.3). Many American parents, for example, would see the familiar in this Bloemenheim mother's account of a child wanting to "do things by oneself":

> Often, when she gets dressed, and for example she brings her socks to me and asks, "Should I put these socks on?" She asks me that. And I help her, just without thinking. And then she has her socks on, and then she sees that and she gets angry and then the socks have to be taken off. . . . "Do self!" And then she begins all over with everything! A bow that I just put on, a T-shirt that I just dressed her in, also have to come off. Then you have to start completely over again [Interview 221-1-59].

Being able to play alone, or entertain oneself, is a second expression of independence recognized by both the Cambridge and Bloemenheim parents, but the Bloemenheim parents highlighted this more (see also Super and oth-

**Table 2.3. Sample Differences in Meaning of "Independent" Behavior**

| Meaning | Bloemenheim (Percentage) n = 16 | Cambridge (Percentage) n = 11 | Chi-Square | p <= |
|---|---|---|---|---|
| Doing things by oneself | 43 | 45 | 0.008 | n.s. |
| Entertaining oneself | 38 | 9 | 2.74 | .10 |
| Making one's own decisions | 19 | 27 | 0.27 | n.s. |
| Having one's own will | 31 | 27 | 0.049 | n.s. |
| Asserting oneself in oppositional way | 6 | 64 | 10.30 | .001 |
| Problem for parents | 0 | 55 | 11.22 | .001 |
| Conflict of independence versus dependence | 0 | 45 | 8.93 | .003 |

Note: n.s. = not significant.

ers, 1996). A mother in Bloemenheim summarized this as part of what she thought being "independent" (*zelfstandig*) means:

> Independence. I think that everyone must be independent. And I have the idea myself that you don't have to push them to be that way. Playing alone outside is independent. Doing a puzzle by yourself is independent. Making a mess and cleaning it up yourself is independent. So, it all belongs together [Interview 220-1-106].

Other aspects of independence mentioned by parents in both communities include making one's own decisions and having one's "own mind" or "own will." Thus parents in both Cambridge and Bloemenheim generally recognized similar kinds of behavior as relevant to the concept of independence, although the Bloemenheim parents focused more on being able to entertain oneself as a developmental goal.

As with dependence, however, there is a striking difference between these two groups of parents in the significance they attached to independence as a developmental and relationship issue. The Cambridge parents typically saw the development of independence as involving an internal struggle on the part of children, torn between wanting to cling to their parents and wanting to strike out on their own. This perspective is evident in the comments of two mothers in particular (one the mother of a three-year-old girl, the other of an eighteen-month-old girl). One of these mothers explained:

> And Courtney is at a point where she really likes my company. "I want some company." So on one hand she wants to be grown up and do things on her

own, but on the other hand she wants to make sure you're there. And so I get that a lot during the week. It's just hard [Interview 108-4-180].

The other said regarding her own daughter:

Well, I think it's—in terms of her developing independence, she feels a very strong need to assert herself. Whenever I feel I have to put a limit on her, I feel she's developing more of an understanding of that. That's a big process she has to sort out in her mind. I think partly the better she feels about herself, also the more scared she gets about growing up and leaving babyhood behind [Interview 130-2-82].

In contrast, the Bloemenheim parents presented a view of children's oppositional behavior as a natural maturational process of discovering one's selfhood. One mother explained her three-year-old daughter's frequently saying "no":

Well, I think she is discovering her own self. That she is also an "I," she is also a person who lives here. That she can do things with the family, but she's discovering her own will. A person who can say, "I want milk" or "I don't want milk" [Interview 221-1-54].

The Bloemenheim parents encouraged this development, as it laid a foundation for the ability later in life to make one's own decisions rather than being too strongly influenced by others. One father described the importance of being independent:

Then he will go his own way and will therefore feel better about himself, I think. If you just try to follow others because you think that they have it better or that others do. How should I say? Independent people attract others to them. And I don't want him to follow after others, I want him to decide what he wants. And then he'll be more comfortable with himself, I think. I do that also. I'm always a bad listener to others. Or at least, I listen well, but then I always follow my own will. And I hope he'll be that way too [Interview 220-1-115].

## Dependence and Independence: The Cultural Contrast

To summarize the themes in the Cambridge and Bloemenheim parents' talk about dependence and independence in their young children, it appears that parents in both settings recognized the same kinds of behavior as relevant to each construct. Dependence was defined as seeking attention and love, and the concept of independence included wanting to do things oneself, having one's own will, and being able to entertain oneself. The two groups of parents diverged sharply, however, in their interpretations of such behaviors and in their attitudes and responses. Whereas the Bloemenheim parents found young children's need for attention and love natural, legitimate, and generally not a burden to themselves, the Cambridge parents worried about whether dependent behavior might be the result of some negative experience and felt torn between wanting to be attentive parents and feeling hassled by their children's excessive demands. Ironically, the Cambridge parents also found independence to entail difficult relationship issues in a way that the Bloemenheim parents did not.

Why did the two groups of parents differ so much in their interpretations of and responses to what were evidently perceived as very similar—indeed probably universal—aspects of behavior in their young children? To address this question, we turn to a reexamination of the basic constructs of independence and interdependence as they have been conceptualized in Western psychology, and in the process we revisit the parallel concepts of individualism and sociocentrism.

## Individualism, Sociocentrism, and the "Autonomous-Relational Self"

Kagitçibasi (1996) has proposed a new synthesis of what she sees as the two dimensions of autonomy inherent, but not recognized, in Western conceptualizations: agency and separateness. "Given this individualistic orientation [of the Western world]," she argues, "autonomy is often construed as separateness from others. Even though autonomy does not necessarily imply distancing oneself from others, such a meaning is commonly attributed to it. It is seen to result from a separation-individuation process and to reflect the differentiation of the self from 'the other.' Independence and separateness appear as prerequisites for autonomy. From such a perspective, therefore, an interdependent self construal would exclude autonomy" (Kagitçibasi, 1996, p. 180). Furthermore, Kagitçibasi proposes, the two dimensions of autonomy are paralleled by two meanings in the construal of individualism versus sociocentrism (or "collectivism," in her terms), wherein collectivism is supposed to entail both subordination of one's own self to the group and emotional closeness or interdependence. She suggests that, in contrast to this confounding of two logically separate dimensions, in some societies (notably those in transition from traditional to individualistic family lifestyles) there is a "dialectical synthesis" involving close emotional relationships but allowing for individual agency. According to this interpretation, the "autonomous relational self" not only is adaptive in certain socioeconomic situations but also provides a healthier solution to the basic human need for both connectedness and agency than do prevailing Western psychological theories.

Although Kagitçibasi draws her examples of the autonomous relational self from outside the Western world, her conceptualization corresponds remarkably closely to the differences observed in the ways that the Cambridge and Bloemenheim parents talked about dependence and independence in their children. For the Cambridge parents, the conflict inherent in both dependence and independence has to do with separation. Although the conflict is attributed to the child, parents also may experience conflict over the presupposed necessity of separation, assumed to be necessary in order for the child to achieve a solid sense of agency. For the Bloemenheim parents, on the other hand, emotional closeness and interdependence are valued, and independence is seen as related mainly to the development of agency—being able to make one's own choices. Note that in the last Dutch example quoted above (Interview 220-1-115), the alternative to being able to make one's own decisions is to be a follower of others; nowhere does the issue of separateness arise.

With the idea of the autonomous relational self in mind, we can more easily make sense of the other differences between Cambridge and Bloemenheim parents' descriptions that appear anomalous in the framework of individualism versus collectivism. Attribution of obedience to children is rare in both samples, although manageability and cooperativeness are definitely issues. The low profile for obedience in these settings reflects the fact that neither is a traditional society in which obedience and respect are highlighted. As Kagitçibasi (1996) notes, obedience (lack of personal agency) is adaptive in traditional societies, characterized by the extended family and a household-based economy, but these constraints on the individual's need for agency are not necessary in modern societies. On the other hand, the higher frequency of "strong-willed" and "enterprising" among Dutch parents as descriptions of their children reflects the strong emphasis on agency in that society. The reasoning behind this seems to be that in Holland, where people live so close together and cannot avoid dealing with each other, parents find it important that one know what one wants in order not to be manipulated by others. However, one cannot be too strong minded because to maintain a peaceful society (long a Dutch priority), other people have to be taken into consideration. Similarly, the ability to make one's own choices and take the initiative, expressed in the descriptor "enterprising" (ondernemend), is a vital component of personal agency in a densely social environment.

Although Kagitçibasi's conceptualization of the autonomous relational self appears to correspond well to the Bloemenheim parents' cultural model of the child as expressed in their descriptions of their own children, it is notable that Kagitçibasi also assumes that such a model can be found only outside Western societies. Are we to imagine, then, that Dutch communities such as Bloemenheim are rare deviants from an otherwise hegemonic "Western mind"? Only further research within the broad bounds of Western culture can answer this question. It seems likely, however, that such research will show that there is not one "Western mind" but many culturally structured ways of conceptualizing the self, and thus of thinking about children and the family. This should be reassuring to both researchers and parents: although each formulation creates its own internal tensions, it also opens the door for more viable solutions to the basic human needs for personal achievement and autonomy as well as sociability and relatedness.

## References

Edwards, C. P., Gandini, L., and Giovaninni, D. "The Contrasting Developmental Timetables of Parents and Preschool Teachers in Two Cultural Communities." In S. Harkness and C. M. Super (eds.), *Parents' Cultural Belief Systems: Their Origins, Expressions, and Consequences.* New York: Guilford Press, 1996.

Geertz, C. "From the Native's Point of View." In R. A. Shweder and R. A. LeVine (eds.), *Culture Theory: Essays on Mind, Self and Emotion.* New York: Cambridge University Press, 1984.

Greenfield, P. M., and Cocking, R. R. (ed.). *Cross-Cultural Roots of Minority Child Development.* Mahwah, N.J.: Erlbaum, 1994.

Harkness, S., and Super, C. M. "Parental Ethnotheories in Action." In I. E. Sigel, A. V. McGillicuddy-DeLisi, and J. J. Goodnow (eds.), *Parental Belief Systems: The Psychological Consequences for Children.* (2nd ed.) Mahwah, N.J.: Erlbaum, 1992.

Harkness, S., and Super, C. M. (eds.). *Parents' Cultural Belief Systems: Their Origins, Expressions, and Consequences.* New York: Guilford Press, 1996.

Kagitçibasi, Ç. "The Autonomous-Relational Self: A New Synthesis." *European Psychologist,* 1996, *1*, 180–186.

Kohnstamm, G. A., Halverson, C. F., Jr., Havill, V., and Mervielde, I. "Parents' Free Descriptions of Child Characteristics: A Cross-Cultural Search for the Developmental Antecedents of the Big Five." In S. Harkness and C. M. Super (eds.), *Parents' Cultural Belief Systems: Their Origins, Expressions, and Consequences.* New York: Guilford Press, 1996.

Super, C. M., Harkness, S., van Tijen, N., van der Vlugt, E., Fintelman, M., and Dijkstra, J. "The Three R's of Dutch Childrearing and the Socialization of Infant Arousal." In S. Harkness and C. M. Super (eds.), *Parents' Cultural Belief Systems: Their Origins, Expressions, and Consequences.* New York: Guilford Press, 1996.

Whiting, B. B., and Edwards, C. P. *Children of Different Worlds: The Formation of Social Behavior.* Cambridge, Mass.: Harvard University Press, 1988.

*SARA HARKNESS is professor in the School of Family Studies and director of the Center for the Study of Culture, Health, and Human Development at the University of Connecticut.*

*CHARLES M. SUPER is professor and dean in the School of Family Studies at the University of Connecticut.*

*NATHALIE VAN TIJEN holds a master's degree in developmental psychology from the University of Leiden and is now a doctoral student at the Free University of Amsterdam.*

**3**

*Intergroup and intragroup variations in Anglo and Puerto Rican mothers' long-term socialization goals and in mother-infant interactions provide an empirical context for this exploration of how we can simultaneously represent both homogeneity and heterogeneity in cultural communities.*

# Homogeneity and Heterogeneity in Cultural Belief Systems

*Robin L. Harwood, Axel Schölmerich, Pamela A. Schulze*

The past several years have seen an increased interest in situating the study of children within cultural contexts (Corsaro and Miller, 1992; Goodnow, Miller, and Kessel, 1995; Rogoff, Mistry, Goncu, and Mosier, 1993). Along with this concern has come a heightened consideration of appropriate conceptual frameworks for studying culture within the larger field of psychology. In particular, interpretive approaches have been articulated among several researchers (Cole, 1996; Harkness and Super, 1996; Shweder, 1996). Despite their diversity, interpretive approaches generally share the assumption that human beings construct meaning through their cultural symbol systems, with language being one of culture's most powerful symbol systems. Many of these approaches go on to assert that this construction occurs in a matrix of social interaction, in which the child as participant actively produces and reproduces culturally meaningful patterns of beliefs and behaviors (see, for example, Schieffelin and Ochs, 1986; Rogoff, Mistry, Goncu, and Mosier, 1993). As interpretive approaches become more widely used, certain themes appear to recur and to demand continued refinement. One particularly salient question involves the issue of how we can understand both homogeneity and heterogeneity of beliefs in a given cultural community.

## Heterogeneity and the Boundaries of a Cultural Community

Shweder (1996, p. 20) defines culture as: "'a reality lit up by a morally enforceable conceptual scheme composed of values (desirable goals) and causal beliefs (including ideas about means-ends connections) that is

This research was made possible through a grant to the first author from the National Institute of Child Health and Human Development (HD32800).

exemplified or instantiated in practice.' Members of a culture are members of a moral community who work to coconstruct a shared reality and who act as though they were parties to an agreement to behave rationally within the terms of the realities they share." This definition is one that many contemporary cultural psychologists can agree with and use as a starting point for their own theoretical and empirical reflections. One issue this definition leaves unaddressed, however, is that of boundaries: To what extent do meanings or "realities" need to be shared among a group of people before we consider that two individuals belong to "the same cultural community"? For instance, can we consider Americans as a whole to be a cultural community? If not, does it make sense to produce any broad generalizations regarding the individualism (or other proposed characteristic) of American culture? Alternatively, do we need a narrower, "less heterogeneous" social group in order to speak meaningfully of cultural communities? If so, then how do we decide what constitutes a "more homogeneous" social group?

For instance, we can consider Yale University faculty and students as constituting a "cultural community," whose members share "a morally enforceable conceptual scheme composed of values (desirable goals) and causal beliefs (including ideas about means-ends connections) that is exemplified or instantiated in practice." On closer inspection, however, we can further subdivide Yalies into more precise groups: Yalies who are actively involved in Hillel House appear to constitute a different group than Yalies who are actively involved in the Latino Studies Center, or Yalies who are members of an elite men's singing group, or even Yalies who are members of the Divinity School or of the psychology department. This is further complicated, of course, by the fact that none of these groups is mutually exclusive.

The question is, to what extent does each of these groups develop its own "morally enforceable conceptual scheme" within Yale, and to what extent does each share in a larger "Yale culture"? Can Yale itself be viewed as sharing with a handful of select universities a "morally enforceable" Ivy League "conceptual scheme instantiated in practice"? Analogously, do we view America as a vast land teeming with countless "subcultures," or do we view all those subcultures as also sharing in a larger, identifiable American "culture"?

In short, any so-called cultural community will, on closer inspection, be composed of smaller and smaller subcommunities, each contributing what appears to be heterogeneity to the larger whole. (Even Yalies in Hillel House or in the psychology department will point to differences among themselves.) Some researchers have argued that this heterogeneity of beliefs in any designated cultural group makes it difficult to characterize culture "at broader levels" (Lightfoot and Valsiner, 1992). On the other hand, it could be argued that, in order to eliminate heterogeneity completely, we would have to consider each community as consisting of a single individual. Conversely, it is difficult to escape the perception that cultures as a whole differ from one another. A day spent in Delhi and a day spent in

Houston will provide both the casual traveler and the serious ethnographer with the impression that, taken as a whole, Houston and Delhi are two very different places, with culturally distinct and discernible patterns of being. We are thus left with a paradox: Cultural communities can be viewed as broad, discernible wholes; cultural communities comprise narrower and narrower, seemingly heterogeneous, subcommunities. How are we to understand this paradox?

A consideration of the term "shared conceptual schemes" may provide us with some insight into this paradox. Definitions of culture as "shared discourse," shared "scripts" for the understanding of self and other, or shared "norms" for social interaction imply a relatively fluid definition of what constitutes a cultural community (Schwartz, White, and Lutz, 1992). A person may simultaneously be a member of multiple groups, each with its own particular "morally enforceable conceptual scheme instantiated in practice." For instance, people may share values and practices regarding belief in a higher power through participation in a religious group at the same time that they share values and practices regarding the pursuit of knowledge through participation in an academic community. Conversely, any cultural community is composed of individuals who also participate in multiple other cultural communities. According to this approach, a cultural community may be viewed not as a bounded, static entity, but as a group of individuals who coconstruct a shared reality in one or more domains of life and who involve themselves in discourse and activities appropriate to an agreed-on level of commonality (Harwood, Miller, and Lucca Irizarry, 1995).

By definition, this level of commonality represents a shifting continuum. At the broadest, most inclusive level, we are all human beings who must confront the issues inherent in physical survival, procreation, and group life. At the narrowest, most exclusive level, we are each absolutely unique individuals. In between these extremes are differing levels of commonality, each with their concomitant markers and appropriate levels of shared discourse and practice. Despite intragroup variability, most Americans know generally how to conduct themselves around each other as polite strangers (not necessarily an easy task outside of one's own native country). For example, a movie theater may be viewed as a cultural setting in which large cross sections of Americans who are generally strangers to one another demonstrate that they share a "morally enforceable conceptual scheme instantiated in practice" regarding appropriate goals and behaviors in this setting: one stands in line to buy tickets; one does not talk or shout comments during the movie; it is permissible to save seats for others; one does not sit right next to a stranger unless no other seats are available; one removes a crying infant from the theater; and so on.

Similarly, despite disparate backgrounds, most Americans share a belief in the importance of individual freedom, self-fulfillment, and upward mobility as major life aims (Spence, 1985). Within these broad parameters, most Americans also maintain numerous other group memberships, entailing more narrow levels of shared discourse and practice, based on geographic region, ethnicity, religion, political affiliation, gender, age, marital and parental status, sexual orientation, occupation, education, and avocation, among other things. For instance, undergraduate members of a small academic community may demonstrate shared norms regarding movie-viewing behavior at their college film festival (complete with shouted comments and communal hissing, groaning, laughter, and applause) that differ from the shared norms they exhibit in practice at a public movie theater. The individuals may be the same, the settings may be arguably similar, but the identified markers of commonality are different, and this transforms these settings into events unique to their particular cultural communities. Our personal identities are thus multiple and overlapping; we are simultaneously members of both a larger U.S. culture and a variety of smaller subcultures within that larger culture. What changes as we move among these groups is not our cultural identities, but the markers we use to delineate the level of discourse and practice appropriate to the situation we find ourselves in.

From this perspective, "heterogeneity versus homogeneity" becomes less compelling as an issue. Individuals will generally adjust their discourse and behavior to an appropriate level of commonality (assuming that they are members of the group in question, share an understanding of appropriate discourse and practice, and are motivated to demonstrate that membership by acting on those norms). The cultural communities composed of those individuals will tend to exhibit both general agreement regarding broad defining constructs and internal variation regarding certain particulars. What is of primary interest is not the ultimately arbitrary boundary we draw to define the cultural community in question but what we can learn about the level of shared discourse and practice among those we have chosen to include as members of the same cultural community (Harwood, Miller, and Lucca Irizarry, 1995; Harwood and others, 1996).

At the level of national membership, it is useful to recall that some concepts (such as "individualism" versus "sociocentrism") appear to be more central as broad cultural constructs, eliciting more conformity to expressed beliefs regarding desirable developmental end points (Goodnow, 1988). It is equally enlightening, however, to examine how specific subcommunities use these broad cultural constructs to inform their own discourse and practice in locally distinctive ways.

## National Group Membership and Socioeconomic Status as Multiple Cultural Communities

What happens when a person belongs simultaneously to two cultural communities that appear to embody competing values and practices? One consistent finding with regard to the study of social class influences on parental beliefs has been that, in the United States, working-class parents tend to place a relatively greater value than do middle-class parents on obedience or conformity to authority, whereas middle-class parents tend to place a relatively greater value on initiative and self-direction. Moreover, these different values are instantiated in different child-rearing practices (Hoff-Ginsberg and Tardif, 1995; Kohn, 1977).

Once again, we confront a paradox. American culture as a whole is said to be individualistic, yet working-class parents in the United States appear to be "less individualistic" in their child-rearing values and practices by virtue of their relatively greater focus on conformity to authority. Similarly, as this pattern of socioeconomic differences manifests itself in countries besides the United States (Kohn, 1977), we might hypothesize that, in a more "sociocentric" culture such as India or Puerto Rico, middle-class parents would appear to be "less sociocentric" than working-class parents, by virtue of their relatively greater focus on initiative and self-direction. How then can we understand the relationship between membership in a national cultural community versus membership in a socioeconomic status group, when these appear to offer competing socialization goals? What does it mean to be a dual participant in two potentially conflicting cultural communities?

One possibility is that the multiple cultural communities in which we all participate provide competing "voices," or cultural schemes, which we are then free to choose among or to combine in idiosyncratic ways. Some working-class parents may choose a more generally "individualistic" schema, whereas others may choose a more traditionally "working-class" schema, and still others may generate novel individual solutions, thus providing a source for "intragroup variability" and making it difficult to draw any broad-level characterizations of either "working-class" or "American" parents.

Alternatively, we may conceptualize national group membership as a broad-level cultural community in which all native-born citizens share and participate. More specific, localized cultural communities (such as those based on socioeconomic status) may be viewed as nested within that larger community. If members of different socioeconomic status groups also share in a larger U.S. culture, then one might reasonably ask whether broad cultural values of individual freedom, self-fulfillment, and upward mobility undergo specific transformations among these different groups. Does the shared discourse of American individualism take on more narrow meanings among subcommunities in the United States? In other words, rather than idiosyncratic solutions to multiple competing conceptual schemes, we may find coherent transformations of the broader cultural scheme in the more localized community. Smaller cultural communities may be viewed as nested within and reacting to larger cultural communities rather than as existing alongside them as equal influences.

From this perspective, we could hypothesize that the conformity to authority demanded by working-class U.S. parents cannot be equated with the sociocentrism said to represent a broad cultural construct among Puerto Rican mothers, any more than a greater emphasis on self-direction among middle-class Puerto Rican mothers can be equated to the individualism said to be characteristic of the broader American culture. Instead, broad cultural constructs are transformed into differing but recognizable patterns by the more localized cultural communities. The coherence of the broad cultural construct is preserved even in the face of internal variation.

This hypothesis finds support in the work of several psychologists who have studied working-class U.S. children and adults in recent years. Miller (1982), for instance, documents the way in which three working-class Baltimore mothers attempt to instill in their two-year-old daughters skills of self-assertion and standing up for oneself, as well as learning how to control hurt feelings and getting one's needs met. Although these developmental goals are comparable to those expressed by middle-class American mothers (Harwood, 1992), the means—teasing, sometimes to the point of tears—was not. Similarly, Strauss (1992) describes how her working-class male interviewees "easily verbalized the values that underpin the 'American dream': with hard work anyone in America can get ahead, and everyone should strive to do so" (p. 199); yet the realities of day-to-day economic struggle rendered the security of a steady paycheck that would feed and house their families a greater motivating force in these men's lives than was the lure of personal success and advancement.

It is thus possible that the greater emphasis on conformity to authority among working-class U.S. parents represents not a long-term goal that competes with more individualistic goals but a different understanding of either: (1) how one achieves the same goals; or (2) how that long-term goal will be instantiated in adulthood, given the realities of the local community.

## Middle-Class and Working-Class Anglo and Puerto Rican Mothers

Previous work by Harwood and colleagues (Harwood, Miller, and Lucca Irizarry, 1995; Harwood and others, 1996) has demonstrated some of the ways in which middle- and working-class Anglo[1] mothers living in New Haven, Connecticut, and middle- and working-class Puerto Rican mothers living in San Juan, Puerto Rico, exist simultaneously in two cultural communities with apparently competing socialization goals (one based on socioeconomic status and the other on national group membership). It was hypothesized that cultural constructs consonant with a characterization of U.S. culture as individualistic and Puerto Rican culture as sociocentric would be generated by mothers across socioeconomic status boundaries in each national membership group, suggesting that broad group memberships can constitute important cultural communities and thus meaningful levels of cultural analysis. Further, it was proposed that socioeconomic status in each national membership group functions as a more localized cultural community, producing specific transformations of the broad-level constructs.

In this previous work, eighty mothers of children ages twelve to twenty-four months were interviewed regarding their long-term socialization goals. Mothers' responses in these interviews were coded into five mutually exclusive content categories (Harwood, 1992; Harwood, Miller, and Lucca Irizarry, 1995):

*Self-maximization* (self-confidence, independence, development of one's talents)
*Self-control* (ability to curb negative impulses toward greed, egocentrism, and aggression)
*Lovingness* (friendliness, warmth, ability to maintain close emotional bonds)
*Decency* (ability to meet basic societal standards for decency, such as being a hardworking, honest person who does not use drugs)
*Proper demeanor* (respectfulness, acceptance by the larger community, appropriate performance of role obligations)

Analyses indicated that both culture and socioeconomic status were contributing significantly to group differences in mothers' long-term socialization goals (Harwood, Miller, and Lucca Irizarry, 1995; Harwood and others, 1996), particularly with regard to the categories of self-maximization and proper demeanor. In general, Anglo mothers used the category of self-maximization more than Puerto Rican mothers did, and in each group middle-class mothers used it more than lower-class mothers. The opposite was true of the category of proper demeanor.

**Individualism Among Middle-Class and Working-Class Connecticut Mothers.** The category of self-maximization as used by the Anglo mothers in these studies (Harwood, Miller, and Lucca Irizarry, 1995) broadly encompasses three dimensions of behavior, all of which are close to the heart of what is usually meant by a characterization of U.S. culture as individualistic: independence, self-confidence, and personal achievement. These individualistic values emerged as a major theme for both the working-class and the middle-class Anglo mothers. They were conceptualized by the working-class mothers, however, from a somewhat different perspective. In particular, for many of the working-class mothers, the concern for self-maximization seemed to grow out of an acute awareness that this is what constitutes the "American dream"—a dream that they themselves had not achieved but that they nonetheless hoped their children would. For many mothers, this was expressed as a desire that their children "go further" in school than they had ("learn to speak and write better than me"), in order to attain the "smarts and money" needed to "get ahead" in life. Concomitantly, other long-term goals besides those related to self-maximization appeared to achieve greater salience in conjunction with the perception that "getting ahead" was potentially problematic. In particular, the working-class Anglo mothers placed greater emphasis than did their middle-class counterparts on becoming a good and decent human being.

**Proper Demeanor Among Middle-Class and Working-Class Puerto Rican Mothers.** As described in Harwood, Miller, and Lucca Irizarry

(1995), proper demeanor in Puerto Rico is intrinsically contextual; it is, by definition, knowing the level of courtesy and decorum required in a given situation in relation to other people of a particular age, sex, and social status. The cardinal rule governing interpersonal interactions in Puerto Rican culture is *respeto,* or respect, which will manifest itself differently depending on the context (Lauria, 1982).

A second crucial dimension of proper demeanor is that it is public. Your ability to maintain proper demeanor defines who you are as a person and how others will respond to you. The positive evaluation of others is a prerequisite to good standing in the community and necessary to survival. The person who lacks the ability to maintain proper demeanor is *un malcriado*—one who has been poorly brought up. Such people are likely to suffer rejection by the larger community.

The concern among the Puerto Rican mothers in these studies that their children display proper demeanor cut across social classes. However, it is interesting to note that whereas among Anglo mothers the category containing culturally valued qualities associated with individualism was expressed at the highest rate among middle-class mothers, among Puerto Rican mothers the category containing culturally valued qualities associated with a more sociocentric orientation was expressed at the highest rate among working-class mothers.

We speculated earlier that the harsher socioeconomic realities of working-class Anglo mothers' lives may make the attainment of culturally valued individual success more problematic; moreover, as individual success becomes more illusory, other goals (such as good behavior in childhood and personal decency in adulthood) may gain greater salience in comparison. There is no comparable argument, however, to make among the Puerto Rican mothers. Proper demeanor does not seem to be either more easy or more difficult to achieve by one group or the other. For instance, none of the Puerto Rican mothers spoke wistfully of how they wish they could have had more of an opportunity to learn *respeto* when they were young or hoped that their children might have more of it than they do. Similarly, no one Puerto Rican group expressed a greater or lesser awareness than the other group that *respeto* is needed to survive in their world. Puerto Rican mothers of differing social classes seemed acutely aware of this, and the importance and difficulties of instilling *respeto* in children were expressed by both groups.

What does seem to distinguish the middle-class from the working-class Puerto Rican mothers is the working-class mothers' more single-minded focus on the category of proper demeanor. Fully two-thirds of the working-class Puerto Rican mothers' responses fell into the category of proper demeanor; the second greatest percentage of responses (15 percent) fell into the category of decency. In contrast, the middle-class Puerto Rican mothers' responses fell into the category of proper demeanor just over one-third of the time, with the rest of their responses spread fairly evenly among three other categories.

**Socioeconomic Status and National Group Membership as Cultural Communities.** In conclusion, although class variability was obtained in this study in the direction hypothesized by Kohn (1977), class differences appear to take shape in culturally specific directions. Working-class Anglo mothers have experienced the difficulty of attaining the upwardly mobile success characteristic of the "American dream." A greater emphasis on good behavior in childhood and decency in adulthood may reflect salient socioeconomic factors in their lives and may also be an attempt to define for themselves a somewhat different, more attainable standard of personal worth.

Unlike their Anglo counterparts, working-class Puerto Rican mothers appear to experience no dissonance between the culturally valued qualities associated with a more sociocentric perspective and what motivates their daily lives. In fact, they use the category of proper demeanor at a far higher rate than do the middle-class Puerto Rican mothers. What distinguishes the two Puerto Rican groups is not that the working-class mothers must reconcile major cultural values with the socioeconomic realities of their lives but that the middle-class mothers make greater use of other categories—those focused more on the individual and the individual's internal life (self-maximization, self-control, and lovingness). It therefore appears that socioeconomic status functions in both the Anglo and Puerto Rican groups as a locus for the transformation of broad cultural constructs into more specific group concerns and that these transformations reflect an awareness of and a patterned response to broad-level cultural constructs.

## Homogeneity and Heterogeneity: Situational Effects

It has long been acknowledged in the psychological literature that different situations elicit different behaviors from the same individual. In fact, recognition of situational effects served historically to modify the usefulness of personality traits as a framework for understanding and predicting human behavior (Bem and Funder, 1978; Mischel and Peake, 1982). At times, the current debate regarding the utility of ascribing broad-level constructs to differing cultural groups is reminiscent of what was once the person-situation debate in social psychology. In particular, terms like "individualistic" and "sociocentric" appear to be perceived by some researchers as constructs akin to personality traits. In response, these researchers have been quick to point out instances where, for example, American mothers emphasize cooperation and Japanese or Indian parents provide their children with choice (Mines, 1994; Nucci, 1994). In a sense, these researchers highlight the difficulty of generalizing within a group across situations and across differential individual responses with regard to cultural meaning systems. Intragroup variability, from this perspective, would seem larger than intergroup variability, undermining the usefulness of broad-level cultural constructs like "individualism" and "sociocentrism." What is emphasized instead is that every cultural group contains within it concepts of both the individual and the group, and these concepts stand ready to be activated among specific persons given the right circumstances.

At this point, it may be useful to reframe this debate regarding intra-group versus intergroup variability in cultural meaning systems by viewing the central question as one of *patterning* rather than one of presence versus absence. For example, to say that American culture tends to be "individualistic" is not to say that concepts like loyalty, commitment, self-sacrifice, and group belonging are absent among Americans. Similarly, to say that Puerto Rican culture tends to be "sociocentric" is not to say that concepts like personal choice, independence, or economic self-sufficiency are lacking among Puerto Ricans. What matters from this perspective is not the absolute presence or absence of a given concept but its patterning in relation to other relevant constructs. To use a more mundane example, the colors blue and red may both be present in two different rugs; however, if blue is in the foreground of one but in the background of the other, the overall visual impact of these rugs is quite different.

To say that American culture is individualistic does not imply that individualism will always be evident or that it will evidence itself in exactly the same way across situations. Instead, we would expect to find situational differences in the ways broader cultural goals are expressed. For example, Pachter and Dworkin (1996) studied mothers' perceptions of infant developmental milestones among socioeconomically diverse Anglo, Puerto Rican, and African American mothers living in Hartford, Connecticut. They found that, consistent with a greater emphasis on independence, both the Anglo and African American mothers expected social and self-care milestones to occur at an earlier age than did the Puerto Rican mothers—with the exception of toilet training. In this case, the Anglo mothers expected their children to achieve toilet training at an average age of two and a half years, whereas the Puerto Rican mothers expected this milestone by eighteen months of age. We are thus left with an exception to the general push among the Anglo mothers toward earlier achievement of social milestones when it comes to the specific situation of toilet training.

However, if we examine the popular American parenting literature, we find coherence rather than contradiction with regard to the reasons given for early self-feeding versus late toilet training. Consider the following quotes from two popular parenting books:

> Whom do you listen to? Does your mother know best? Or Doctor? . . . Actually, your baby does—nobody can tell you when to start giving your baby solids better than he or she can. . . . To decide if your baby is ready for the big step into the world of solid foods . . . look for the following clues [Eisenberg, Murkoff, and Hathaway, 1989, pp. 202–203].

> Learning acceptable toilet behavior is much more difficult for children than learning sensible eating or even sleeping habits, because the toilet behavior that is asked of them has no obvious reward. . . . If you try to insist on coop-

·eration before your child is emotionally ready, you will be trying to impose your will on the toddler's [Leach, 1994, p. 219].

From this perspective, both early self-feeding and late toilet training become situationally specific instantiations of the belief that children should exercise choice over what happens to their own bodies. In one case, this manifests itself as the right to choose the rate and type of food consumption at an early age; in the other case, it manifests itself as the right to delay meeting societal expectations regarding elimination until the child is "emotionally ready." Situational variability occurs—but as a patterned response to the larger cultural goal of promoting individual agency.

## Cultural Patterning and Situational Variability: Middle-Class Anglo and Puerto Rican Mothers

To begin to examine empirically the possibility that we may find cultural patterning in situational variability, we focused in a more recent study on middle-class Anglo mothers in northeastern Connecticut ($n$ = 22) and middle-class Puerto Rican mothers in San Juan, Puerto Rico ($n$ = 18). In both settings, mothers of firstborn infants twelve to fifteen months old were recruited from pediatricians' offices, from day-care centers, and by word of mouth. Mothers met the following criteria: formal schooling beyond high school; and white-collar or professional household occupational status, as determined by Hollingshead's four-factor scale (1975).

**Participants.** In Connecticut, mothers were white (of non-Hispanic European ancestry), had been born in the United States, and spoke English as their first language; mean educational achievement was 16.5 years, and mean household Hollingshead score was 53.3, or near the boundary between minor and major professional. Seventy-eight percent of the Connecticut mothers worked outside the home for an average of 32.1 hours per week, and mean maternal age was 31.5.

In San Juan, mothers had been born, reared, and educated on the island and spoke Spanish as their first language. Puerto Rican mothers averaged 15.9 years of formal schooling and had a mean household Hollingshead score of 50.9. Seventy-eight percent of the Puerto Rican mothers worked outside the home for an average of 37.3 hours per week, and mean maternal age was 27.9. Analyses of variance indicated that group differences arose on just one demographic variable: as found in previous studies (Harwood, Miller, and Lucca Irizarry, 1995; Harwood and others, 1996), middle-class Anglo mothers were older on average than middle-class Puerto Rican mothers ($p < .05$). Both groups thus represented a highly educated, professional group of mothers. It is also worth noting that Puerto Rico's status as a commonwealth of the United States makes socioeconomic status across these two settings more comparable than is normally the case in cross-cultural studies.

**Procedure.** As in previous studies, mothers were questioned regarding their long-term socialization goals ("What qualities would you like to see your child come to possess? What qualities would you *not* like to see your child come to possess?"), and their responses were coded into the same five content categories (self-maximization, self-control, lovingness, decency, and proper demeanor) used in previous research (Harwood, 1992; Harwood, Miller, and Lucca Irizarry, 1995; Harwood and others, 1996).

In addition, mothers were videotaped interacting with their infants in a variety of everyday situations (feeding, social play, teaching, and free play with toys) for standardized amounts of time (ranging from five to ten minutes). The videotaped mother-infant interactions were coded in real time using Interact software (Dumas, 1993), which computes the frequency of different types of behaviors and the duration of different types of settings. In our mother-infant interactions, we chose to code the following: frequency of different types of maternal nonverbal and verbal behaviors common across the situations; and frequency and duration of selected maternal behaviors that were specific to each situation.

**Results: Long-Term Socialization Goals.**  Mothers' responses to the questions regarding their long-term socialization goals showed a pattern similar to the one obtained with previous middle-class Anglo and Puerto Rican mothers (Harwood, 1992; Harwood, Miller, and Lucca Irizarry, 1995). In particular, the analysis of variance indicated that, compared with Puerto Rican mothers, Anglo mothers were more likely to generate responses falling into the combined categories of self-maximization and self-control (respective means = 5.89 and 9.95, $p < .05$) and less likely to generate responses falling into the combined categories of proper demeanor and decency (respective means = 9.17 and 3.82, $p < .01$). This is consistent with an emphasis on individualistic goals among the Anglo mothers and an emphasis on sociocentric goals among the Puerto Rican mothers.

**Results: Mother-Infant Interactions.**  Analyses of variance indicated that mothers' verbal and nonverbal behaviors toward their infants were consistent with the broad cultural constructs of individualism among the Anglo mothers and sociocentrism among the Puerto Rican mothers. However, culturally patterned situational variability arose with regard to these results in two primary ways.

First, as expected, cultural goals manifested themselves somewhat differently across the different settings (see Table 3.1). In general, Puerto Rican mothers were more active and directive than were Anglo mothers in structuring their infants' behaviors, but this manifested itself somewhat differently according to the situation. In particular, compared with the Anglo mothers, the Puerto Rican mothers were more likely to

- Signal their infant's attention (all four situations)
- Physically position their infants (teaching only)
- Physically restrain their infant's free movement around the room (social play only)
- Issue direct commands to their infants (feeding, teaching, and free play)

Similarly, in general, the Anglo mothers encouraged their infants to show more personal choice and active freedom than did the Puerto Rican mothers. Again, however, there was situational variability in precisely how this manifested itself. In particular, Anglo mothers were more likely to

- Phrase their directives as suggestions (social play, teaching, and free play)
- Explicitly praise their infant's actions (feeding, teaching, and free play)

In this way, both groups of mothers demonstrated coherence between their professed long-term socialization goals and the ways in which they organized their interactions with their infants in these four everyday situations. It is important to note, however, that the instantiations of these cultural goals varied somewhat according to the situation.

**Table 3.1. Mean Frequency of Maternal Verbal and Nonverbal Behaviors**

| Behavior | Anglo | Puerto Rican | p |
|---|---|---|---|
| Feeding | | | |
| Signaling infant's attention | 1.73 | 9.72 | * |
| Commanding | 2.68 | 13.67 | ** |
| Suggesting | 7.23 | 10.67 | |
| Affection | 0.55 | 0.89 | |
| Praise | 3.64 | 0.61 | * |
| Social play | | | |
| Positioning infant | 2.36 | 3.72 | |
| Restraining infant's movements | 1.55 | 5.11 | ** |
| Signaling infant's attention | 1.18 | 6.28 | ** |
| Commanding | 6.82 | 10.28 | |
| Suggesting | 5.73 | 2.83 | * |
| Affection | 1.18 | 1.50 | |
| Praise | 1.64 | 0.56 | |
| Teaching | | | |
| Positioning infant | 0.90 | 2.44 | * |
| Restraining infant's movements | 1.81 | 2.56 | |
| Signaling infant's attention | 14.81 | 37.11 | ** |
| Commanding | 21.67 | 34.33 | * |
| Suggesting | 28.38 | 6.94 | ** |
| Affection | 0.86 | 3.17 | * |
| Praise | 9.33 | 4.83 | ** |
| Free play | | | |
| Positioning infant | 0.91 | 1.0 | |
| Restraining infant's movements | 0.55 | 1.28 | |
| Signaling infant's attention | 7.45 | 16.0 | ** |
| Commanding | 9.82 | 26.22 | ** |
| Suggesting | 19.59 | 3.61 | ** |
| Affection | 1.32 | 3.0 | |
| Praise | 4.82 | 1.28 | ** |

*p < .05.
**p < .01.

Second, as expected, each of the four settings produced unique opportunities for interaction; however, mothers appeared to respond to these situational opportunities in culturally specific ways (see Table 3.2). In particular, Anglo mothers were more likely to encourage their infants to self-feed, whereas Puerto Rican mothers were more likely to spoon-feed their twelve- to fifteen-month-old infants. During social play, Puerto Rican mothers spent significantly more time playing games with their infants requiring social coordination, like touching and turn-taking games. Setting-specific cultural differences also arose during free play, with Anglo mothers more likely to sit back while their infants played alone and less likely to try to structure their infant's attention by attempting to engage the infant with toys of their own selection.

## Discussion

In conclusion, we find evidence of heterogeneity in cultural groups, both in terms of different subcommunities within a larger national culture and in terms of situational variability within the same group. In both cases, however, the heterogeneity was culturally patterned. In subcommunities defined by middle- and working-class socioeconomic status, we found that the broader cultural values did not disappear but were transformed in ways that were

## Table 3.2. Mean Frequency of Situationally Specific Maternal Behaviors

| Behavior | Anglo | Puerto Rican | p |
|---|---|---|---|
| Feeding | | | |
| Offering food (spoon-feeding) | 8.36 | 41.94 | ** |
| Encouraging self-feeding | 7.64 | 1.39 | ** |
| Infant feeding self | 23.82 | 2.78 | ** |
| Social play (mean duration in seconds) | | | |
| Clapping games | 15.59 | 31.29 | |
| Bouncing games | 22.23 | 25.55 | |
| Hiding/chasing games | 35.05 | 15.41 | |
| Touching/turn-taking games | 20.18 | 49.76 | * |
| Teaching | | | |
| Guiding infant's hand | 3.19 | 7.89 | |
| Demonstrating task for infant | 29.86 | 29.56 | |
| Infant trying task on his or her own | 11.33 | 11.17 | |
| Offering target object to infant | 3.52 | 9.0 | ** |
| Free play (mean duration in seconds) | | | |
| Mother and infant playing together | 190.64 | 181.94 | |
| Mother watching infant play | 207.68 | 125.28 | ** |
| Mother shifting infant's attention | 7.64 | 25.44 | * |
| No play activity | 37.5 | 61.89 | |

$*p < .05.$

$**p < .01.$

meaningful to each socioeconomic group. For the Anglo working-class mothers, this meant a greater fear that individual dreams of success would not be met and a greater concomitant tendency to find alternative ways of defining and measuring personal worth. In Puerto Rico, the middle-class mothers were less single-minded than were the working-class mothers in their focus on cultural values of *respeto* and proper demeanor. This may reflect either: a functional tendency for middle-class parents to focus more on the individual because they are in jobs that require greater self-direction, as Kohn (1977) suggested; or cultural change in Puerto Rico, with the more highly educated, professional mothers beginning to embrace less-traditional values.

We also found cultural patterning in the instantiation of broad cultural constructs when examining mother-infant interactions in four everyday situations. In particular, Puerto Rican mothers generally engaged in a greater degree of active structuring of their infants' behaviors than did Anglo mothers. However, this manifested itself differently across the different situations (for example, Puerto Rican mothers' greater use of physical restraint during social play and of physical positioning during teaching). Moreover, mothers made culturally patterned uses of the specific opportunities for interaction afforded by the different situations (for example, Anglo mothers' greater encouragement of self-feeding and greater tendency to sit and watch their infant play alone during free play). Thus, although mothers did not behave identically across all four situations, they did behave in ways that were consistent with larger cultural goals and expectations.

Rogoff, Mistry, Goncu, and Mosier (1993, p. 1) suggest that "development occurs through active participation in cultural systems of practice in which children, together with their caregivers and other companions, learn and extend the skills, values, and knowledge of their community." Consistent with this, our findings indicate that mothers' long-term socialization goals reflect larger cultural belief systems. Intragroup variations in these goals, such as those relevant to differences in socioeconomic status, appear to represent transformations of larger cultural beliefs into more specific, localized group concerns. In addition, mothers structure their interactions with their infants in ways that are generally consistent with their long-term socialization goals. Children thus engage repeatedly in situationally specific instantiations of larger cultural values in a variety of everyday settings. Situationally appropriate behavior is itself culturally patterned, further illustrating the ways in which homogeneity and heterogeneity can coexist coherently in a larger cultural belief system.

### Note

1. *Anglo* has a long history of use as a cultural term contrasting the English-speaking Americas with the Spanish-speaking Americas. We will therefore use the term *Anglo* to describe the white American women of non-Hispanic European ancestry who participated in this study.

## References

Bem, D. J., and Funder, D. C. "Predicting More of the People More of the Time: Assessing the Personality of Situations." *Psychological Review*, 1978, *85*, 485–501.

Cole, M. *Cultural Psychology: A Once and Future Discipline.* Cambridge, Mass.: Harvard University Press, 1996.

Corsaro, W. A., and Miller, P. J. (eds.). *Interpretive Approaches to Children's Socialization.* New Directions for Child Development, no. 58. San Francisco: Jossey-Bass, 1992.

Dumas, J. *Interact Software System, V. 2.0.* West Lafayette, Ind.: Purdue University, 1993.

Eisenberg, A., Murkoff, H. E., and Hathaway, S. E. *What to Expect the First Year.* New York: Workman, 1989.

Goodnow, J. J. "Parents' Ideas, Actions, and Feelings: Models and Methods from Developmental and Social Psychology." *Child Development*, 1988, *59*, 286–320.

Goodnow, J. J., Miller, P. J., and Kessel, F. (eds.). *Cultural Practices as Contexts for Development.* New Directions for Child Development, no. 67. San Francisco: Jossey-Bass, 1995.

Harkness, S., and Super, C. M. (eds.). *Parents' Cultural Belief Systems: Their Origins, Expressions, and Consequences.* New York: Guilford Press, 1996.

Harwood, R. L. "The Influence of Culturally Derived Values on Anglo and Puerto Rican Mothers' Perceptions of Attachment Behavior." *Child Development*, 1992, *63*, 822–839.

Harwood, R. L., Miller, J. G., and Lucca Irizarry, N. *Culture and Attachment: Perceptions of the Child in Context.* New York: Guilford Press, 1995.

Harwood, R. L., Schölmerich, A., Ventura-Cook, E., Schulze, P. A., and Wilson, S. P. "Culture and Class Influences on Anglo and Puerto Rican Mothers' Beliefs Regarding Long-Term Socialization Goals and Child Behavior." *Child Development*, 1996, *67*, 2446–2461.

Hoff-Ginsberg, E., and Tardif, T. "Socioeconomic Status and Parenting." In M. H. Bornstein (ed.), *Handbook of Parenting*, Vol. 2: *Biology and Ecology of Parenting.* Hillsdale, N.J.: Erlbaum, 1995.

Hollingshead, A. B. *Four Factor Index of Social Status.* Unpublished manuscript, Yale University, 1975.

Kohn, M. L. *Class and Conformity: A Study in Values.* (2nd ed.) Chicago: University of Chicago Press, 1977.

Lauria, A. "*Respeto, Relajo,* and Interpersonal Relations in Puerto Rico." In F. Cordasco and E. Bucchioni (eds.), *The Puerto Rican Community and Its Children on the Mainland.*(2nd ed.) Metuchen, N.J.: Scarecrow Press, 1982.

Leach, P. *Your Baby and Child from Birth to Age Five.* New York: Knopf, 1994.

Lightfoot, C., and Valsiner, J. "Parental Belief Systems Under the Influence: Social Guidance of the Construction of Personal Cultures." In I. E. Sigel, A. V. McGillicuddy-DeLisi, and J. J. Goodnow (eds.), *Parental Belief Systems: The Psychological Consequences for Children.* (2nd ed.) Mahwah, N.J.: Erlbaum, 1992.

Miller, P. J. *Amy, Wendy, and Beth: Learning Language in South Baltimore.* Austin: University of Texas Press, 1982.

Mines, M. *Public Faces, Private Voices: Community and Individuality in South India.* Berkeley: University of California Press, 1994.

Mischel, W., and Peake, P. K. "Beyond Déjà Vu in the Search for Cross-Situational Consistency." *Psychological Review*, 1982, *89*, 730–755.

Nucci, L. "Mothers' Beliefs Regarding the Personal Domain of Children." In J. G. Smetana (ed.), *Beliefs About Parenting: Origins and Developmental Implications.* New Directions for Child Development, no. 66. San Francisco: Jossey-Bass, 1994.

Pachter, L. M., and Harwood, R. L. "Culture and Child Behavior and Psychosocial Development." *Journal of Developmental and Behavioral Pediatrics*, 1996, *17*, 191–198.

Rogoff, B., Mistry, J., Goncu, A., and Mosier, C. "Guided Participation in Cultural Activity by Toddlers and Caregivers." *Monographs of the Society for Research in Child Development*, 1993, *58*(236).

Schieffelin, B. B., and Ochs, E. (eds.). *Language Socialization Across Cultures.* New York: Cambridge University Press, 1986.

Schwartz, T., White, G. M., and Lutz, C. A. (eds.). *New Directions in Psychological Anthropology.* New York: Cambridge University Press, 1992.

Shweder, R. A. "True Ethnography: The Lore, the Law, and the Lure." In R. Jessor, A. Colby, and R. A. Shweder (eds.), *Ethnography and Human Development: Context and Meaning in Social Inquiry.* Chicago: University of Chicago Press, 1996.

Spence, J. T. "Achievement American Style: The Rewards and Costs of Individualism." *American Psychologist,* 1985, *40,* 1285–1295.

Strauss, C. "What Makes Tony Run?: Schemas as Motives Reconsidered." In R. D'Andrade and C. Strauss (eds.), *Human Motives and Cultural Models.* New York: Cambridge University Press, 1992.

*ROBIN L. HARWOOD is assistant professor in the School of Family Studies at the University of Connecticut.*

*AXEL SCHÖLMERICH is professor of developmental psychology at Martin Luther University in Halle-Wittenburg, Germany.*

*PAMELA A. SCHULZE is a doctoral student in child and adolescent development in the School of Family Studies at the University of Connecticut.*

4

*The expressed values of European American and Latino children, their parents, and their teachers reveal the multifaceted nature of individualistic and collectivistic conceptions of relationships and the varied ways in which cultural value conflict may be manifested in children's daily developmental settings.*

# Conceptualizing Interpersonal Relationships in the Cultural Contexts of Individualism and Collectivism

*Catherine Raeff, Patricia Marks Greenfield, Blanca Quiroz*

Contemporary American society is characterized by contact among people who enact different cultural values about interpersonal relationships in varied settings. As cross-cultural psychologists began to explore cultural dimensions of human behavior, individualism and collectivism were identified as useful constructs for theory and research concerning different cultural values about the self and relationships (Hofstede, 1980; Triandis, 1989). Initially, there was a tendency to view individualism and collectivism as unidimensional and dichotomous constructs. However, recent work in this area indicates that individualism and collectivism are complex and multifaceted value systems that reflect different historically constituted standards for the interplay between independence and interdependence (Raeff, 1997). The individualism and collectivism constructs can be useful for understanding different cultural values about relationships, but more information is needed about these value systems and how their different conceptions of relationships are particularized in children's daily lives.

We thank the participating children, parents, and teachers; our teacher collaborators, Ana Serrano and Marie Altchech; our research assistants, Mirella Benitez, Sae Lee, Patricia Morales, Rachel Ostroy, Kenichi Sakai, Claudia Torres, and Hedwig Wölfl; and Anne Raeff for translation assistance. This research was supported by the UCLA Urban Education Studies Center. Earlier versions of this chapter were presented to the Society for Research in Child Development in 1995 and to the International Society for the Study of Behavioral Development in 1996.

In psychology, individualism has typically been defined in terms of independence (Greenfield, 1994; Markus and Kitayama, 1991), deriving from the central assumptions that human beings are ideally free and of equal status. Some theorists tend to view these assumptions as antithetical to interdependence (Sampson, 1988), thus ignoring the way relationships are structured and conceptualized in individualistic societies. In contrast, we start from the position that human beings, from any culture, are embedded in social relationships and that human development takes place in relation to others. Thus, we seek to consider how the individualistic assumptions of freedom and equal status shape the structuring of relationships.

Modern American individualism emerged during the eighteenth century out of Western liberal traditions in political and social philosophy. Democracy was viewed as the most viable political system for ensuring national unity while simultaneously preserving the liberty of all citizens. In this framework interpersonal relationships are typically defined contractually, and they may be explicitly negotiated in terms of the choices and goals of individual participants. Because previous views of individualism have emphasized the value of independence, these relational aspects of individualism have been neglected in psychology.

Previous work has defined collectivism in terms of interdependence and the central assumption that human beings are primarily members of groups (Triandis, 1989). Whereas individualism views group membership and social relationships ideally in terms of choice and mutual consent, collectivism treats social relationships as links that, ideally, establish interdependence and reciprocal obligations. Based on the priority of group membership, the self and relationships tend to be defined in terms of responsibilities that are inherent in the nature of relationships and in terms of mutually understood social roles, particularly within one's in-group (for example, one's family). Fulfilling social roles and responsibilities preserves and promotes the group's welfare, and the group's welfare also represents the welfare of its individual members. Thus, promoting social goals both maintains the social order and enhances the individual. Social roles are often organized in hierarchical terms (Delgado-Gaitan, 1994), but insofar as all group members are integral to social functioning, individuals and their social roles are considered to be of equal importance for maintaining and promoting the group's welfare. Collectivism is favored in agrarian societies and has been prevalent in varied non-Western cultures (Greenfield and Cocking, 1994).

## European American and Latino Conceptions of Relationships

Because individualism and collectivism have different implications for the structuring of relationships, conflict can arise between them when they come into contact. Currently in the United States many minority and immigrant children come from cultural backgrounds that are rooted in collectivistic traditions (Greenfield and Cocking, 1994). Previous research shows that European Americans tend to favor individualism, whereas Latinos from Mexico and Central America tend to favor collectivism (Delgado-Gaitan, 1994). An orientation toward collectivism is particularly characteristic of the immigrant generation. As Latino children and their families come into contact with American individualistic conceptions of relationships, especially through the children's public school attendance, cultural value conflict may occur (Greenfield, Raeff, and Quiroz, 1996; Quiroz and Greenfield, in press). By exploring how European American and Latino children, parents, and teachers conceptualize relationships, this study will elucidate how conflict about appropriate modes of interacting with others may be manifested in school settings.

**Expectations, Questions, and Design.** As a first step in systematically studying conceptions of relationships and areas of cultural value conflict, scenarios involving interpersonal dilemmas were presented to European American and Latino children, to their parents, and to the teachers in the children's schools. It was expected that there would be two distinct ways of resolving these dilemmas, reflecting individualistic and collectivistic conceptions of relationships.

By including parents as well as teachers, it is possible to explore how immigrant children and their families may be struggling with the values of their collectivistic home cultures and the individualistic values of the public schools. In particular, this study was conducted in two different elementary schools in Los Angeles. School 1 served a primarily European American population, and School 2 served a primarily immigrant Latino population. Cultural value agreement among children, parents, and teachers, reflecting common individualistic values, was expected at School 1. In contrast, varied forms of cultural value conflict were expected at School 2, including value conflict between collectivistic parents and individualistic teachers. Value conflict between the children with collectivistic backgrounds and their individualistic teachers could also arise. And finally, there could be value conflict between the collectivistic parents and their children, as the children acculturate and begin to construct more individualistic conceptualizations of relationships. It was also expected that teachers of varied ethnicities would express generally individualistic values due to acculturation, formal education, and teacher training.

In addition to interviewing male and female child participants, we designed scenarios in two versions: one with female child characters and the other with male child characters. These gender variables were included because of questions concerning the role of gender in conceptions of relationships. Gilligan (1982) distinguished between a "care orientation" that is typically characteristic of females and a "justice orientation" that is typically characteristic of males. This perspective suggests that there would be differences in how males and females solve the scenario dilemmas and that all participants might respond differently to the scenarios based on the gender of the scenario characters.

However, Miller (1994) argues that Gilligan's concept of a caring orientation reflects individualistic assumptions because it is based on individual choice, in contrast to the social duty orientation that is characteristic of collectivism. According to Miller's perspective, one would expect differences between Latino and European American participants rather than differences between male and female participants or differences based on scenario characters' gender. Manipulating the gender of the scenario characters permits analyses of whether the participants' expressed values reflect Gilligan's or Miller's analysis.

**Samples and Methods.** The samples came from two elementary schools in the Los Angeles metropolitan area. School 1 was a private, university-affiliated elementary school. Participants from School 1 included twenty European American fifth-grade children (nine girls, eleven boys) and sixteen of their mothers. Fourteen of the mothers were American-born, one mother had immigrated from Ireland and completed college in the United States, and one mother had immigrated from South Africa after completing her education. The range of educational level among these mothers was 13 to 20 years (mean educational level = 16 years). There were fifteen teachers from this school, including eleven European Americans, two African Americans, and two Mexican Americans (one was born in the United States, and one had immigrated thirteen years before).

School 2 was an urban public school. Participants from School 2 included twenty-eight Latino fifth-grade children (sixteen girls, twelve boys). The children's parents were immigrants, and the children ranged from having been born in the United States to having immigrated one year ago (mean time in the United States = 6 years). The children were mostly of Mexican heritage (82 percent Mexican, 7 percent Guatemalan, 4 percent Nicaraguan, 7 percent Salvadoran). From School 2, nineteen immigrant parents of the fifth-graders also participated in the study, including seventeen mothers, one father, and one grandfather who was the child's primary caregiver. The range of time living in the United States for the parents was 2 to 20 years (mean time in the United States = 10 years). The parents were primarily Mexican immigrants (90 percent Mexican, 5 percent Nicaraguan, 5 percent Salvadoran). The range of educational level among these parents was 0–12 years (mean educational level = 5 years). Finally, sixteen teachers from School 2 participated in the study, including twelve European Americans, one African American, two Latinos (one was born in the United States, and one had immigrated twenty years before), and one Asian American (born in the United States).

Clearly, cultural differences cannot be separated from differences in educational level in the two parental samples. However, based on the assumption that individualism and collectivism constitute broad cultural constructs that can be enacted in different ways by various groups in a culture (see Chapter Three in this volume), the current sample of Latino participants is taken to be representative of the collectivistic values enacted by many immigrant Latino families who now populate urban American schools, particularly in California and the Southwest. The current sample of European American participants is taken to be representative of mainstream American individualistic values that Latino immigrants encounter as they participate in varied sociocultural settings, including school.

**Materials.** Open-ended hypothetical scenarios that describe children in interpersonal situations at home and at school were designed. The scenarios were based on observations of conflict situations involving Latino children in school, on observations of European American schoolchildren, and on the reported experiences of immigrant families. There was a total of eight scenarios; four involved home situations, and four involved school situations. To elucidate individualistic and collectivistic relationship themes, this chapter includes data from two home scenarios and two school scenarios that emphasize the structuring of interpersonal relationships.

**Procedure.** There were two random orders of presentation. For each scenario order, there was a version with only female names and a version with only male names, totaling four sets of scenarios. Names that could be used in either English or Spanish were selected. The scenarios were translated into Spanish, using the method of back translation, so that participants could choose to have the scenarios presented in either Spanish or English. In School 2, twenty-one of the twenty-eight Latino children and all of the Latino parents chose to participate in Spanish. The scenarios were presented orally to all participants individually, and all sessions were audiotaped. All of the children were interviewed in person, at their schools. The parents were interviewed in person or by telephone, depending on what made them feel most comfortable. Fifteen European American parents were interviewed over the telephone, and one was interviewed in person. Eighteen Latino parents were interviewed in person, and one was interviewed over the telephone. All of the teachers were interviewed in person at their schools.

After the presentation of each scenario, participants were asked an open-ended question about how the scenario's interpersonal dilemma should be resolved. After the participants gave their initial responses, they were asked why they thought this was the best way to handle the situation. This open-ended question was designed to probe the participants' personal constructions of meaning in relation to cultural values.

For each scenario, coding categories were derived from the data, and they encompass both the initial responses and the participants' justifications. A multicultural research team (including European Americans and Latinos) contributed to constructing the categories and to interpreting their central relationship themes. To assess interrater reliability for these categories, 21 percent of the English protocols were coded independently by three coders. Two of these coders also spoke Spanish, and they coded an additional 5 percent of the protocols to include the interviews that were conducted in Spanish. Using Cohen's kappa coefficient, interrater reliability ranged from .78 to .96.

The research team also classified each category as individualistic (I), collectivistic (C), or as reflecting aspects of both individualism and collectivism (I&C). Participants' responses for each scenario received an I, C, or I&C score (I = 0, I&C = .50, C = 1.0), resulting in a mean individualism-collectivism (I-C) score for each participant, ranging from 0 to 1.0. Using this scale, means near 0 are relatively individualistic, means near .5 indicate a mixture of the two value orientations, and means near 1.0 are relatively collectivistic.

**Statistical Analyses and Hypotheses.** Two levels of data analyses were conducted. First, to analyze overall scores on the I-C dimension, analyses of variance (ANOVAs), using school and role (child, parent, or teacher) as the independent variables, were conducted on the participants' I-C scores. It was hypothesized that there would be an interaction between role and school. The hypothesized interaction was expected to yield differences in expressed values among parents, teachers, and children in School 2 (Latino families) but not in School 1 (European American families). In School 2, we expected parents to be more collectivistic in their value orientation than the teachers, with children falling in between their parents and teachers. In School 1, we expected all three groups to fall on the individualistic side of the scale.

Looking at the interaction in another way, we also expected increasing differences between expressed values at the two schools as one moved from teachers (no differences between schools), to children (Latino children slightly more collectivistic than European American children), and to parents (Latino immigrant parents significantly more collectivistic than European American parents). The hypothesis that the teachers' responses would reflect individualistic values, despite ethnic variation among the teachers, was also tested.

Second, in order to understand how the different scenarios were construed and resolved as reflections of cultural values about the structuring of relationships, responses to each scenario were analyzed separately. These analyses of the participants' construction of meaning will be presented for three scenarios that illustrate the overall patterns of results and that pertain to different individualistic and collectivistic relationship themes.

## Results and Discussion

In accord with our hypothesis, there was a significant two-way interaction between school and role: $F (2, 2) = 4.51, p < .01$. With respect to differences in each school, $t$ tests showed that there were no significant differences among the children, parents, and teachers at the European American school, and as hypothesized, all three groups fell on the individualistic end of the scale. However, as predicted, there was cultural value conflict at School 2, with significant differences between the Latino immigrant parents and the teachers: $t (33) = 4.28, p < .001$; significant differences between the children and the teachers: $t$ (42) = 2.65, $p$ < .011; and significant differences between the children and their parents: $t$ (45) = −2.48, $p$ < .017. Latino immigrant parents and their children were more collectivistic than the teachers, and Latino immigrant parents were also more collectivistic than their children.

Whereas the teachers did not differ in the two schools, the Latino parents and children tended to be more collectivistic than the European American parents and children. The mean I-C score for the Latino parents at School 2 was .63, and the mean I-C score for the European American parents at School 1 was .27. Results of $t$ tests revealed a significant difference between the parents at the two schools: $t$ (33) = −5.02, $p$ < .001. The mean I-C score for Latino children at School 2 was .46, and the mean I-C score for the European American children at School 1 was .33; $t$ tests showed that these differences were not significant. These results for the children and the parents at the two schools confirm the expectation that the differences between the children would be smaller than the differences between the parents. The mean I-C score for the teachers at School 1 was .24, and the mean I-C score for the teachers at School 2 was .29, indicating that the teachers at both schools were generally individualistic. In $t$ tests it was confirmed, as hypothesized, that there were no significant differences between the European American and non–European American teachers.

An ANOVA indicated that there was an effect for scenario order: $F$ (4, 1) = 10.67, $p$ < .001; but there were no interaction effects between scenario order and school or between scenario order and role. Consequently, it was reasonable to collapse across orders in the statistical analyses, as in the ANOVAs reported earlier. Paired $t$ tests showed that there were no differences in the participants' responses to the home and school scenarios, indicating that value orientations did not differ by scenario setting.

Regarding gender, an ANOVA comparing all participants' I-C scores by gender of participant and gender of scenario characters yielded no main effects and no interaction effects for the two factors. Thus, the participants' responses support the predictions based on Miller's theory of culture rather than Gilligan's theory of gender differences.

These overall analyses provide general confirmation for the expectations regarding differential expressions of individualism and collectivism for the children, parents, and teachers at the two schools. However, qualitative analyses of individual scenarios are required to explore the substance of individualistic and collectivistic conceptions of relationships and to explore how cultural value agreement and conflict are particularized in relation to specific relationship issues.

## Individual Scenario Analyses

Each scenario and the coding categories will be presented with either female or male names. The most common responses will be presented, and all reported results will be depicted graphically.

*SCENARIO 1: JOBS. It is the end of the school day, and the class is cleaning up. Denise isn't feeling well, and she asks Jasmine to help her with her job for the day, which is cleaning the blackboard. Jasmine isn't sure that she will have time to do both jobs. What do you think the teacher should do?*

For this scenario, the following two coding categories encompassed 82 percent of the participants' open-ended responses:

1.  *Find third.* The teacher should find a third person to do Denise's job. There were four subcategories indicating different justifications for this core category. The subcategories were coded as individualistic because the main goal is to protect Jasmine from the burden of helping the other child without her explicit consent or agreement, so that she can complete her own task.
    a.  *Find third to excuse the sick child.* "Well if I were the teacher I think I'd probably . . . see if there were some other child who would volunteer to help the child who isn't feeling well to do the blackboards" (teacher, School 2).
    b.  *Find third to protect Jasmine's task.* "Give the work to another pupil. Because the teacher has to understand that the pupil can't do the two things at the same time because [she] doesn't know if [she] has time" (child, School 2).
    c.  *Find third to ensure that all jobs are completed.* "I think the teacher needs to find somebody else that can also help them and maybe if we divide up Denise's job then there will be time to get everything done" (teacher, School 2).
    d.  *Find third for a combination of the above reasons.* "Is there someone else who can help Denise, who isn't feeling well? Because it's being sensitive to Denise's feelings, emotions, and also sensitive to Jasmine so she is not overwhelmed by her duties" (teacher, School 1).
2.  *Help.* The teacher should tell Jasmine to help Denise. This category was coded as collectivistic because the main goal is to help Denise, without concern for Jasmine's personal preferences or job. "The child should help the girl because she's sick, and she could get sicker" (child, School 2).

The category of finding a third person indicates the importance of finding someone who is not otherwise occupied and agrees to help, as well as the importance of helping others. In this way, help is provided by mutual agreement, and requests for volunteers are explicitly stated. By finding a third person, Jasmine's goals and rights are respected and not infringed upon, and Denise may also receive help. This category reflects the individualistic assumption that, as a free individual, Jasmine has the right to pursue her own goals and to make her own decisions, without external infringement.

The second category, telling Jasmine to help Denise, illustrates the implicit expectation of helping a classmate and friend; it is treated as an automatic social responsibility. This response reflects the collectivistic assumption that human beings are responsible for helping group members in order to contribute to the welfare and unity of the group. From a collectivistic perspective, helping Denise does not constitute an infringement on Jasmine. Instead, it enables Jasmine to fulfill her role in relation to one of her classmates, thus strengthening this particular relationship, which in turn can contribute to her welfare and the welfare of the entire class.

These contrasting conceptions of relationships were distributed differently in the two schools. Sixty percent of the European American children, 63 percent of the European American parents, and 47 percent of the teachers at their school said that the teacher should find a third person. In contrast, 20 percent of the children, 19 percent of the parents, and 20 percent of the teachers said that the teacher should tell Jasmine to help Denise with the job. There were no significant differences among the children, parents, and teachers at School 1, revealing cultural value harmony between European American families and the teachers at their school.

In School 2, 64 percent of the Latino children, 16 percent of the Latino parents, and 50 percent of the teachers thought a third person should be found. In contrast, 36 percent of the Latino children, 74 percent of the Latino parents, and 13 percent of the teachers said that Jasmine should be asked to help Denise with her job. This distribution in the predominantly Latino School 2 shows that cultural value conflict is played out in complex ways. Fisher Exact Tests indicated that the parents were significantly more collectivistic than the teachers ($p = .002$) and that the parents were significantly more collectivistic than the children ($p = .002$). There were no significant differences between the children and the teachers. For this school situation, cultural value conflicts between the teachers and parents, as well as between the children and parents, suggest that the children may be struggling to balance the values of their homes and schools.

SCENARIO 2: T-SHIRT. *Adam and Johnny each get $20 from their mother, and Johnny buys a T-shirt. A week later, Adam wants to borrow Johnny's T-shirt, and Johnny says, "No, this is my T-shirt, and I bought it with my own money." And Adam says, "But you're not using it now." What do you think the mother should do?*

For this scenario, the following two coding categories encompassed 80 percent of the participants' open-ended responses:

1. *Choice or personal property rights.* The mother should tell Adam that it is Johnny's choice because the T-shirt belongs to him. This category was coded as individualistic because the main goal is to protect personal ownership rights and the individual's right to make decisions about one's own property. "I think since he had bought it, then it is his. . . . And if he doesn't want him to wear it, then he shouldn't be able to wear it" (child, School 1).

2.  *Share.* The mother should tell the boys to share. For this category there were two subcategories, reflecting different justifications for the core category. Both subcategories were coded as collectivistic because the solution emphasizes promoting relationships based on implicit expectations.
    a.  *Share to be a good person as a general principle.* "Tell the boy that he should lend it to him. Because they should share" (parent, School 2).
    b.  *Share because they are siblings.* "Let him borrow it. Because they're brothers" (child, School 2).

The "share" category reflects the collectivistic values of sharing for the sake of overall social cohesion and sharing to promote the welfare of the group (in this case, the family) as a whole. This category is compatible with previous research, which shows that the primary value of material goods in a collectivistic framework lies in their capacity for facilitating social relationships. The individualistic "choice or personal property rights" category indicates that because individual rights and personal property are primary, it is Johnny's choice whether he wants to share or not, even though sharing is valued. This category suggests that, in an individualistic framework, the interpersonal activity of sharing is negotiated around individual choice and the mutual consent of the participants.

These conceptions of relationships were played out differently in the two schools. In School 1, 60 percent of the European American children, 81 percent of the European American parents, and 53 percent of their teachers claimed that, because the T-shirt belonged to Johnny, it was his decision whether or not to share. In contrast, 30 percent of the children, 6 percent of the parents, and 13 percent of the teachers said that the mother should tell Johnny to share his T-shirt. Once again, there were no significant differences among the children, parents, and teachers at School 1.

In School 2, 50 percent of the Latino children, 42 percent of their parents, and 69 percent of the teachers said that because the T-shirt belonged to Johnny, it was his decision whether or not to share. Thirty-two percent of the children, 58 percent of the immigrant Latino parents, and 6 percent of the teachers said that the mother should tell Johnny to share his T-shirt. In this case, there was statistically significant value conflict only between the parents and the teachers ($p = .006$), showing again that Latino immigrant parents were more collectivistic than the teachers. It is noteworthy that the children's responses fell in between the responses of the parents and teachers, although they were not significantly different from either their parents or their teachers. Comparing the findings of the first two scenarios, we see that the children depart more from their parents' value system when the scenario setting is school, rather than home.

SCENARIO 3: DINNER. *Jessica is the first one home in the afternoon. When her mother gets home at seven, she finds that Jessica has not started cooking dinner yet. When she asks Jessica why she didn't get dinner started, Jessica says she wasn't hungry. What do you think the mother should do?*

For this scenario, the following two coding categories accounted for 66 percent of the participants' open-ended responses:

1.  *Chore.* If getting dinner was the child's prearranged chore, then she should have done it, and the mother should talk to her about her agreed-upon responsibilities. This category was coded as individualistic because it emphasizes the contractual nature of relationships and social obligations. "If it's her responsibility, then she should explain that it's not a matter of whether she's hungry or not, it's part of what she's been asked to do as a member of the household and the expectation is that she will do it" (parent, School 1).

2.  *Group.* The mother should tell the child she should have thought of the rest of the family and she should have started dinner. This category was coded as collectivistic because the main goal is to emphasize the individual's implicit awareness of other people's needs and to place the needs of others above her own needs and preferences. "Tell her that if she's not hungry, maybe the others are hungry. And since they're going to be coming home from work tired, they're not going to be able to make the meal" (child, School 2).

The "chore" category is in keeping with the individualistic assumption that because people are free and responsible for their own needs, some dimensions of their relationships are explicitly created. Thus, aspects of the child's role in the family can be explicitly created and negotiated. Once established, these roles represent responsibilities to a wider whole that take precedence over momentary individual needs. However, insofar as individual roles in relation to others are explicitly created by the participants, they may be subject to ongoing negotiation based on the changing needs, goals, and choices of the group's individual members. From a collectivistic perspective, the "group" category elucidates the importance of automatic responsibility for contributing to the family unit. This response indicates the value of having an implicit understanding of the group members' goals such that they do not have to be explicitly stated. It is expected that these goals will be anticipated by individuals, who will not only bring value to the group by contributing to family needs but will also be valued for their contributions as group members.

These conceptions of relationships were differentially evident in the two schools. In School 1, 30 percent of the European American children, 56 percent of the European American parents, and 80 percent of the teachers responded according to the "chore" category. At the same time 45 percent of the children, 19 percent of the parents, and 7 percent of the teachers said that Jessica should think of the family or group and should have started dinner. In this case there was a significant difference between the children and the teachers at School 1 ($p = .007$), with the teachers more individualistic than the children. It is possible that this difference reflects a developmental progression whereby European American children at first emphasize automatic helpfulness and are socialized into a more contractual approach to relationships (see, for example, Madsen, 1971).

In School 2, 43 percent of the Latino children, 37 percent of their parents, and 13 percent of the teachers said that Jessica should have thought of the family or group and started dinner. Fourteen percent of the children, 16 percent of the parents, and 44 percent of the teachers said that if it was Jessica's prearranged chore, she should have started dinner. There was agreement among the Latino children and their parents, but there were significant differences between the teachers and the children ($p = .015$), as well as between the teachers and the parents ($p = .046$). Significantly more Latino parents and children, and significantly fewer teachers, thought that Jessica should have started dinner. The children's tendency to respond collectivistically may reflect the preservation of their families' original collectivistic values for dividing labor at home. This division of labor may be contrasted to the division of labor at school as reflected in the Jobs scenario, where the Latino children responded more like their teachers, and significantly more individualistically than their parents.

The participants' responses to the scenarios discussed in this chapter are depicted graphically in Figures 4.1 and 4.2.

**Individualistic Conceptions of Relationships.**  The three scenarios provide information about how the individualistic assumptions that people

**Figure 4.1. Distribution of the European American School 1 Participants' Responses to the Scenarios**

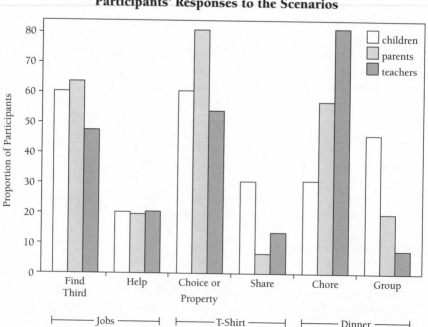

**Figure 4.2. Distribution of the Latino School 2 Participants'
Responses to the Scenarios**

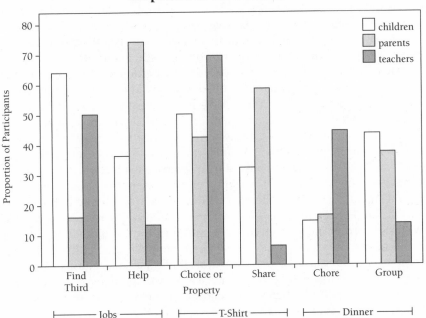

are ideally free are reflected in conceptions of relationships. The Jobs scenario highlights how attention to others is conceptualized in terms of not infringing on their individual goals. The solution of finding a third person to help the sick child demonstrates the importance of not infringing on someone's task or goals while helping another person and of creating relationships in terms of the individuals' choices and goals. Moreover, the Jobs scenario reveals the importance of both receiving and giving help through negotiation, thus going beyond previous approaches to individualism, which have suggested that such attention to others is precluded by the individualistic worldview.

The T-Shirt scenario also reveals that interpersonal interactions and relationships are ideally structured in terms of individual choices and goals in the individualistic framework. The solution that emphasizes the owner's right to choose to share ("choice or personal property rights") indicates how individual and private ownership rights may form the foundation of relationships in which sharing material goods is negotiated between the owner and potential borrower. This scenario also indicates that sharing is a valued dimension of social relationships when it is a matter of individual choice and preference.

In the Dinner scenario, viewing cooking dinner for the rest of the family as a prearranged chore reflects a contractual model of social obligations, and this precondition suggests the importance of negotiation based on the mutual consent of individuals in relation to each other. The "chore" category also shows that when certain individual needs or goals are in conflict with a negotiated and prearranged group social role, the group's interests and personal responsibility for that social role may be emphasized over individual goals.

**Collectivistic Conceptions of Relationships.** The three scenarios also provide information about how the collectivistic assumption that social responses are implicit in the roles of individual group members is reflected in conceptions of relationships. Thus, mutually understood expectations regarding relationships are emphasized in the domain of social behavior. In the collectivistic framework, the "help" category for the Jobs scenario indicates the absolute value of helping. From a collectivistic perspective, this solution is perceived as an opportunity to make or strengthen interpersonal relationships. Moreover, the possibility of exerting extra effort to finish one's own job in order to be able to help a group member is not viewed as an infringement. This view indicates that the primary goal for an individual— that is, for a group member—is to form links with other group members, which in turn promote the welfare of both the group and the individual.

The T-Shirt scenario suggests that, in a collectivistic culture, sharing material goods is an assumed aspect of interpersonal relationships, thus revealing the priority of relationships over private property and individual ownership. It also elucidates how material possessions can serve to facilitate relationships rather than serve as a source of conflict among individuals. Similarly, in the Dinner scenario, cooking dinner for other family members without regard for personal preferences ("group" category) indicates how individual roles within a wider social matrix involve an assumed or implicit awareness of the group's needs and how, therefore, these obligations do not need to be explicitly stated or arranged. In such situations, it is the individual's responsibility to determine how to act in the best interests of the group, thus also promoting the individual's own well-being.

## Cross-Cultural Differences in Value Conceptualization and Intragroup Variability

Based on different conceptions of relationships, the results indicate that there was general cultural harmony among the European American children, their parents, and their teachers. In contrast, there was general cultural value conflict between the teachers and the immigrant Latino families. The findings suggest that these children of Latino immigrants may be struggling to balance the individualistic conceptions of relationships valued by the school with the collectivistic conceptions valued by their families.

These results indicate that when European American families send their children to school, the schools support the parents' goals concerning the development of their children's social relationships and, conversely, that the parents support the school's goals for their children's social development. However, such a situation of mutual support for common developmental goals does not necessarily exist when Latino immigrant parents send their children to school. Instead, the school's ideals concerning the development of social relationships may undermine the parents' goals for their children's social development, and, conversely, the parents may undermine the school's goals for children's social development. These contrasting social developmental goals set up a difficult situation for both families and schools to negotiate, and knowing about these kinds of subtle dynamics may help to build bridges between home and school.

Although the most common solutions for each scenario dilemma distinguish the Latino families from the European American families and the teachers in both schools, there was also variability in each group. For example, some of the Latino parents and children used the "choice or personal property rights" response in the T-Shirt scenario, and some of them used the "chore" response in the Dinner scenario. For the Latino children and parents, these findings may be attributed, in part, to acculturation. It is also possible that individualistic values are making inroads in the immigrants' countries of origin, especially in relation to increasing industrialization, urbanization, and opportunities for formal education in Mexico (Tapia Uribe, LeVine, and LeVine, 1994). With respect to the heterogeneous responses of many participants from the primarily European American School 1, it is possible that there is bidirectional cross-cultural influence between immigrants and the mainstream culture (Rodriguez, 1993).

In addition, if individualism and collectivism are viewed as different cultural systems composed of interrelations among constituent parts, then categories that are ostensibly the same take on different meanings when they are embedded in different systems (Raeff, 1997). For example, in the T-Shirt scenario, sharing is valued in both individualistic and collectivistic cultures, but the differences lie in how sharing is conceptualized, prioritized, and particularized in relation to customary action patterns. Similarly, in the Jobs scenario, highlighting the importance of helping in the collectivistic "help" response should not obscure the importance of helping others in the individualistic "find third" response. However, within the individualistic framework, helping is not conceptualized as an implicit social responsibility, as it is in the collectivistic framework. Thus, helping others may be a common dimension of human social life, but there are differences in the cultural meanings and values regarding how, why, and when help is provided.

Such findings indicate the complexities of individualism and collectivism, showing that they are neither dichotomous value systems nor constituted by mutually exclusive values. Instead, individualism and collectivism are both value systems for the structuring of independence and interdependence, and the differences between them lie in how values regarding social relationships are conceptualized, prioritized, and enacted in everyday contexts. Continuing to explore multifaceted dimensions of cultural value systems in relation to the personal construction of meaning will promote further understanding of the dynamics of culture and development.

## References

Delgado-Gaitan, C. "Socializing Young Children in Mexican-American Families: An Intergenerational Perspective." In P. M. Greenfield and R. R. Cocking (eds.), *Cross-Cultural Roots of Minority Child Development*. Mahwah, N.J.: Erlbaum, 1994.

Gilligan, C. *In a Different Voice*. Cambridge, Mass.: Harvard University Press, 1982.

Greenfield, P. M. "Independence and Interdependence as Developmental Scripts: Implications for Theory, Research, and Practice." In P. M. Greenfield and R. R. Cocking (eds.), *Cross-Cultural Roots of Minority Child Development*. Mahwah, N.J.: Erlbaum, 1994.

Greenfield, P. M., and Cocking, R. R. (eds.). *Cross-Cultural Roots of Minority Child Development*. Mahwah, N.J.: Erlbaum, 1994.

Greenfield, P. M., Raeff, C., and Quiroz, B. "Cultural Values in Learning and Education." In B. Williams (ed.), *Closing the Achievement Gap*. Alexandria, Va.: Association for Supervision and Curriculum Development, 1996.

Hofstede, G. *Culture's Consequences*. San Anselmo, Calif.: Sage Press, 1980.

Madsen, M. "Developmental and Cross-Cultural Differences in the Cooperative and Competitive Behavior of Young Children." *Journal of Cross-Cultural Psychology*, 1971, *2*, 365–371.

Markus, H. R., and Kitayama, S. "Culture and the Self: Implications for Cognition, Emotion, and Motivation." *Psychological Review*, 1991, *98*, 224–253.

Miller, J. G. "Cultural Diversity in the Morality of Caring: Individually Oriented Versus Duty-Based Interpersonal Moral Codes." *Cross-Cultural Research*, 1994, *28*, 3–39.

Quiroz, B., and Greenfield, P. M. "Cross-Cultural Value Conflict: Removing a Barrier to Latino School Achievement." In R. Paredes and K. Gutierrez (eds.), *Latino Academic Achievement*. Latino Eligibility Task Force, University of California, in press.

Raeff, C. "Individuals in Relationships: Cultural Values, Children's Social Interactions, and the Development of an American Individualistic Self." *Developmental Review*, 1997, *17*, 205–238.

Rodriguez, R. "Slouching Toward Los Angeles." *Los Angeles Times*, Apr. 11, 1993, pp. M1, M6.

Sampson, E. E. "The Debate on Individualism." *American Psychologist*, 1988, *43*, 15–22.

Tapia Uribe, F.M.T., LeVine, R. A., and LeVine, S. E. "Maternal Behavior in a Mexican Community: The Changing Environments of Children." In P. M. Greenfield and R. R. Cocking (eds.), *Cross-Cultural Roots of Minority Child Development*. Mahwah, N.J.: Erlbaum, 1994.

Triandis, H. C. "The Self and Social Behavior in Differing Cultural Contexts." *Psychological Review*, 1989, *96*, 506–520.

CATHERINE RAEFF *is a former postdoctoral fellow in applied developmental psychology at the University of California, Los Angeles. She is now assistant professor of psychology at Indiana University of Pennsylvania.*

PATRICIA MARKS GREENFIELD *is professor of psychology at the University of California, Los Angeles.*

BLANCA QUIROZ *received her master's degree in Latin American studies from the University of California, Los Angeles. She is now a doctoral student in human development at Harvard University.*

5

*Teachers, it seems, have much more uniform beliefs about "the" child than do parents or students—a fact with implications for the education of all three groups.*

# Uniformity and Diversity in Everyday Views of the Child

*Kelvin L. Seifert*

Too often everyday discussions about children are inconclusive. Interlocutors propose ideas, offer opinions, and describe personal experiences—but where does it all lead? The conversations may create new insights, but often they leave initial ideas unchanged. Communication has not occurred, or at least has not occurred well. We "talk past each other," much of the time even cheerfully and without awareness.

It is this experience—of individuals talking past each other—that motivated the research summarized in this chapter. Miscommunication about children can have important consequences. A parent and teacher may need to discuss a child's difficulties in school, and to do so they must understand each other in ways that are more than superficial. A professor may wish to discuss the nature of human development with students, yet success doing so will depend on the professor's sensitivity to assumptions about human nature that the students bring to class. Spouses may argue, sometimes furiously, about what a child "really needs," but resolving such encounters may require attending less to stated positions than to unstated beliefs about the sort of creature children in general are.

Still, misunderstanding is not universal, and communication does succeed sometimes; individuals may indeed understand each other's opinions and observations, whether about a particular child or about children in general. What accounts for the difference? Why might two parents (or teachers or students) "hit it off" well in talking about children, whereas two others do not? A number of factors contribute to mutual understanding, but one that may be especially important is the implied *root metaphor* in an everyday dialogue— the underlying image or analogy about what the world is like in general and

NEW DIRECTIONS FOR CHILD AND ADOLESCENT DEVELOPMENT, no. 87, Spring 2000  © Jossey-Bass Publishers

75

about what children are like in particular. Work by Pepper (1942) and Lakoff (1987), among others, suggests that metaphorical thinking guides some or even all thinking about a wide variety of topics and activities. Furthermore, research by Super and his colleagues (1996) suggests that metaphorical thinking can guide ideas about child development in particular.

The philosophical analysis by Pepper is especially relevant to understanding how root metaphors might influence reflective thinking in general—and presumably also shape metatheories about development of "the" child. On the basis of extensive analysis, Pepper concludes that all systematic thinking (at least in philosophy) is framed by one of just four possible perspectives, which he calls root metaphors. Each is based on everyday experience but becomes elaborated as it guides the development of ideas on any particular topic or cognitive activity. Because each is based on a distinct image or analogy, the metaphors are essentially incommensurable; it is not possible to discredit one worldview by using the terms of another.

Pepper named the four root metaphors formism, mechanism, contextualism, and organicism. *Formism* is based on the metaphor of similarity of objects and their classification into discrete and hierarchical categories. In this view the world is populated by "types" of things, and true knowledge consists of defining and organizing the bases of similarity among objects, as well as diagnosing where particular objects belong within the categories thus defined. In contemporary psychology, for example, formism is well represented by temperament theory and by the approach of the *DSM-IV* (American Psychiatric Association, 1994). Both are based on taxonomies, in this case of human nature.

*Mechanism* is based on the metaphor of the machine. The world consists of relatively few generic parts (such as atoms) related by relatively few causal laws (such as gravity), but these basics interact in complex ways to produce the diversity of the everyday world. Knowledge consists not of cognition or ideas, but of having effective impact or influence on the environment. A rat in a learning box can therefore be said to "know" how to get food pellets if it repeatedly presses a lever. Verbalizations also count as knowledge, but only if they too produce effects on the environment, including the verbal environment of most human beings. In psychology this sort of view is associated with behaviorism.

*Contextualism* is based on the idea of the unique historical event. Knowledge comes from understanding the full context of an action, including both historical and contemporary actions that may be influential, as well as the meanings assigned to these by the observer. Truth also comes from verifying initial understandings of an event or action through further actions by the observer—a form of philosophical operationalism. In contemporary psychology contextualism is especially prevalent in applied fields, such as progressive education or existentialist psychotherapy.

*Organicism* is based on the idea of the developing organism or system. What is important, however, is not the uniqueness of a particular organism (contextualism emphasizes uniqueness) but the universal, mutual influence and patterning of its parts. Organicism stresses internal regulation and reorganization and notes that parts of a system that seem initially fragmentary may later fuse or integrate into larger, more comprehensive wholes. In psychology this point of view is represented by the work of stage theorists such as Piaget.

How might these metaphors guide everyday thinking about children? There are, of course, many possibilities; I will describe how speculations about the answer to this question might begin. An extreme formist might focus on permanent qualities of the child; intelligence, for example, might seem to be an inborn quality, not one that develops. The mechanist might focus instead on the specifics of what "the" child can do and on how to influence the current stock of skills and behaviors. The contextualist might emphasize the uniqueness of each child and deny that generalizations about children can be made at all. And the organicist might identify stages or phases of childhood and point out how each stage had precursors in behaviors occurring earlier in childhood.

Applied thus, Pepper's root metaphors seem simplistic and too extreme. We might expect most parents to express elements of more than one metaphor or perhaps to frame their beliefs in some other metaphor(s) entirely. But the speculations hint nonetheless at a potential problem in communicating everyday beliefs. Persons who assume different metaphors of "the" child might have trouble understanding each other's comments, perhaps without realizing why. Conversely, they might imagine that they understand each other when in fact they do not. In still other dialogues, persons inclined toward the same or similar metaphors might understand each other well—but perhaps, again, without necessarily knowing why.

Framed with these theoretical possibilities and practical concerns, this chapter discusses research about whether metaphors, like those described by Pepper, lie at the heart of everyday conceptions of "the" child. As will be shown, the results did support the general hypothesis—that implicit metaphors do underlie everyday reflections about children. The metaphors bear some resemblance to the "root" metaphors described by Pepper, but not consistently, and further research will be needed to assess why individuals and groups rely on particular metaphors.

The studies described were part of a research program concerned with the nature of teachers' and parents' beliefs about children and education (Seifert, 1992, 1993, 1994; Seifert and Handziuk, 1993). All used extended individual interviews, transcribed and analyzed for themes and content. Participants were always some combination of parents, experienced teachers, preservice teachers, and students. Across all studies there were, altogether, fourteen students, eleven early childhood teachers, and seven parents (all mothers). Interviews in every case focused on aspects of psychology or child development: the nature of the child ("What do you think children are like in general?") or notions of development ("How do children change as they get older?") and learning ("Are there experiences which you think have special impact on children?"). Details of the methods of interview and analysis are described in the publications cited above. Interviews ranged in number from two to five per individual and from twenty to ninety minutes. Individual participants were selected deliberately for their experiences as university students, early education teachers, or parents.

Although differences in topics and participants obviously created differences in the content of interviews, their analysis explored philosophical themes and dimensions that transcended the individual studies. One common theme, for example, was the ontology of "the" child, or the sort of being a child is thought to be. Another theme was the epistemology of participants—their assumptions and metaphors about the nature of learning and development. This theme was initially framed by the writings of Pepper (1942). In the current review of the interviews, the ontological and epistemological themes are considered together and interpreted in light of the most general work, that of Pepper.

## How Diverse Is "the" Child?

In line with other research on this topic, the four studies found substantial qualitative diversity in most adults' everyday concepts of "the" child. As noted below, however, one group—the experienced early childhood teachers—offered more uniform views than the others. The comparative uniformity of the teachers was unexpected: the interviews in all studies had highlighted individuality of belief, and interpretations had borrowed more from psychological frames of reference (with their focus on differences) than from sociological or cultural frames of reference. Why then did the eleven early childhood teachers seem so similar? This question remains an issue for further research; at the end of this chapter, I will offer ideas to resolve it. First, however, I will describe the extent of the contrast between diversity and uniformity, in everyday metaphorical terms and then in terms of Pepper's root metaphors.

## Parents: Mary Clare and Martha

The seven parents in the studies were uniform only in seeing "the" child as a long-term commitment ("fifty to eighty years of it!" one parent said). Beyond this link, they were eclectic as individuals and diverse as a group in the sort of creature they believed "the" child to be. In Pepper's terms each parent supported more than one of the root metaphors at some point during her interviews, and three parents supported all four of the metaphors.

One mother, for example, described "the" child as an inherent feature of "the" family as a whole, with the child's individuality rather secondary in importance; but another described "the" child as quite autonomous, even when still an infant. The first attitude was conveyed graphically by Mary Clare in the 1992 study:

> I think [being a child] is reaching out into the world, coming back to touch base at home, and reaching out again. As the years go by, they reach further, but never stop coming back. . . . [I remember my infant son] sprawled on the couch. I had towels all over me because he would throw up every time he'd eat. And he had been nursing and he looked up at me with his big, brown eyes, and I knew we were related.

In spite of the implication of these comments, being a child had relatively little to do with age. A child was defined instead by a relationship to particular others, the child's parents. Chronologically, therefore, a "child" could also be an adult:

> The transmission went out the other day. And I was stuck in the middle of town, with the car going nowhere. And who was the first person I called? My father! [laughs] Here I am, over forty, and I'm still calling my daddy to bail me out. He was quite touched by it.

Mary Clare did notice differences between the young and the old; it was just that for her, the differences did not define the essential nature of children, even if they described childhood superficially. For her the essence of childhood was found in a child-family relationship, and speaking of "the" child without reference to family was a contradiction in terms, a semantic category mistake. Even when pointedly asked to define "a child" without reference to its relationships or its age, for example, Mary Clare chose to focus on the neediest time of life, early infancy:

> Well, they are these little beings that come into the world just about as totally helpless as anything you could imagine. . . . They are completely dependent on the parents for everything. . . . As they begin to grow a little bit, it's a two-way street. There's a lot of give and take. They bring a lot to the relationship, and then they also need a lot.

Nor was Mary Clare oblivious to differences among children as individuals. She noted obvious differences in behavior and temperament between her two sons, for example, that seemed beyond the influence of family relationships:

> When Joel and Aram have been doing something [in] such totally different ways or respond to a situation in such totally different ways, you wonder. . . . They were different from the moments they were born. From the first five minutes, I knew we had different children. . . . by the way they held their bodies.

But she found such differences hard to understand, perhaps because they never fit comfortably within her framework of child-in-family. She was never prepared to see sibling differences as simply "in" each sibling individually:

> [My husband and I] have gone around and around on why they are different. I tend to look at "why is it this way?" And "is it something that *we* can do something about?" We ask that a lot, but we just tend to go in circles.

Behind her comments on children, siblings, husbands, and fathers, Mary Clare often implied a belief in philosophical contextualism—a resistance to making generalizations or stating principles that transcend time or space and a preference for assessing persons and actions in light of the current situation, or context. She even denied, for example, that she had any views about children in general:

> I don't know if I've ever thought about [children] as such. I think I probably in day to day life tend to think more in situational terms. As things come up, I think, "OK, what's going on here?"

In this light, it is probably most accurate to say that Mary Clare had neither an "ontology of the child" nor an "ontology of the family" but an ontology of evolving, individualized child-family relationships. Mary Clare's way of thinking tended toward contextualism in Pepper's sense: each child-family relationship was unique, both across time and among individuals. As noted further on, however, she was ambiguous in her commitment and fell short of either expressing or implying a single coherent worldview when talking about children.

Mary Clare differed noticeably from Martha, another parent in the same study. Martha described "the" child as a rather autonomous creature, albeit one whose autonomy developed over the course of its lifetime. At birth a newborn's autonomy centered on its physically alien nature; "they are just grubs," said Martha, for the first several months of life. As infants grow into preschoolers, they of course respond more to parents and peers, but this change heralds not so much social connection as self-centeredness:

> [When they're younger] they're not really aware of being part of any group. They're so self-centered; they're just themselves and the group is taken care of by Mom. When they're older, they're getting ready to move out, wanting to make a break. Younger, they're not really part of [the family]; they're at the center of it. Older, they're away.

Always, for Martha, there is a psychological gap between parent and (infant) child; they are aliens. When asked to define "the" child in general, Martha focused not on a child's need for relationships, as had Mary Clare, but on what a child looks like—a quality that parents can really do nothing about:

> I'd say that children are little people. They look like me or like [their] fathers. So you can recognize them; they're different from trees and dogs and things that walk on four legs. And they're simply shorter and proportioned slightly differently.

Physical nature and physical changes remained part of her meaning of "the" child, even when referring to psychological qualities directly:

> There must be something that's going on in their physical development, in their brain, that allows them to develop self-control. I think it's physiological development, not just social context.

Martha described most developmental changes as if they were cognitive, evolving "in" the child, rather than in social exchanges. For language development, older children "get more words, learn to discriminate grammatical features." Little mention is made of language as communication or as a form of social learning; language seems to be read or imitated directly from culture in general, rather than coconstructed by interlocutors. Likewise for motor skills; if they include a social component, that component does not seem to develop in early childhood:

> The mechanics of eating, that comes first. And they have to learn what goes into what they're eating. Katie [my daughter] will say, "Sammy's spitting on my food again." Well, he's trying it out again to see if it works.

Here Martha alludes to a piece of the social context of eating (sitting with a sibling for a meal), but her emphasis remains on the child as an individual, self-directing learner rather than a community participant. At best, Martha only hinted at social learning as a mechanism of development; she never said, for example, "The family provides a language context for learning when and how to speak" or "Dinnertime gives Sammy a way to see how grown-ups eat and to try using those techniques himself."

The result was to imply autonomy for the child and to minimize parents' ability to influence a child's development. By adolescence, according to Martha, the gap between parent and child becomes obvious and explicit. As she says, "they're trying to make a break with you." But the trend really begins much earlier, in early childhood:

> Those that are happy will probably stay happy; those that are pensive will probably stay pensive; those that are extraordinarily active will always have that in them in some form or another. There are some things about them that won't change.

In terms of Pepper's scheme, Martha, unlike Mary Clare with her contextualist tendencies, spoke from a mixture of organicist and formist epistemologies.

For Martha children develop as self-contained, patterned wholes (organicism), but there are also identifiable "types" of children (formism), whatever their age and whatever their parents' efforts to influence them. Like Mary Clare, however, Martha left important ambiguities in her comments and was not philosophically consistent.

## University Students: Chris and Robin

Like the parents, university students expressed views of the child that were both eclectic and diverse. Although no student described "the" child using all four of Pepper's metaphors, all fourteen used more than one metaphor, with the combinations themselves varying from one student to the next. Chris, for example, described a child as little different from an adult, either cognitively or emotionally (Seifert, 1994). As a thinker, a child uses the same strategies as an adult, and with comparable success:

> [The university text says that at age six] children invent spellings. Well this is not something unique to children. I'm like twenty-seven years old and do the same thing with words I don't know. . . . I don't think a teacher can [help with everything]; the students have to do some learning on their own—probably most of it. . . . Teachers don't sit and go over [the material] during class.

Emotionally, too, a child is vulnerable to stresses in much the same way as an adult:

> [The text says] that the preschool years are critical. . . . But something could happen to me right now, and I'm not in preschool years; but it could affect the way I experience things later in life. . . . An example: an old lady gets her purse snatched while walking down the street. Do you think she'll walk down that street again at night or alone? Or ever again, even?

Socially there seem to be no age-related changes. In one interview, for example, Chris was asked to comment on an anecdote about two sisters' concerns about dressing to "look cool." He acknowledged the sisters' concern but added that it had little to do with their ages:

> [The story shows] that people follow or do what other people expect of them . . . just follow the crowd. Not necessarily young people; it can be adults, too. Like right now, [all of my friends] are going to, say, a certain bar, so everyone wants to go to that bar, because that's where everyone's going. So that's the same as with the two girls [in the story].

The only way in Chris's world that children truly develop is physically. Asked to define "the" child, he focused on their physical changes and likened these to organic growth:

[If I were to define "the" child,] I'd say I'm a person, and I started out, developed and started out, from something smaller. And what I grew from would be a "child." Like a plant starts from a seed.

Underlying Chris's nondevelopmental perspective were beliefs that individuals are fundamentally separate and autonomous, whether they like to be or not. As a student, therefore, "the" child has to navigate through learning experiences alone, despite any urges to get help:

I don't think a teacher can cover every little thing. I think that's part of learning, that students have to do some learning on their own. Probably *most* learning on their own. A lot of the reading and stuff all has to be done at home; [teachers] don't sit and go over it and read the book with you during class or anything like that.

The fundamental separation of individuals from each other creates inevitable disagreements among them. This is noticeable, for example, in conflicts of interest between teachers and students, but Chris broadened his comment to include all human encounters:

I guess some students just want automatically to disagree with whatever's said. Some people are just like that. And again, I think it's not, it doesn't happen to a certain age. It happens all through. They could grow out of it and they could grow into it. Adults could have it [a tendency to disagree].

In making these comments, then, Chris for the most part avoided an organicist metaphor—one that sees the child as changing organically over time. What he believed instead was not clear, although it was probably a mixture of formism and mechanism. Chris in essence equated the child's nature with general human nature, a categorizing task of formism. Yet consistent with mechanism, he highlighted linear causation: specific life events were said to have specific effects. These perspectives were probably at least partially a reflection of his lack of direct experience with children. Unlike parents or teachers, Chris could draw only on his readings (such as psychology textbooks) and on memories of his own childhood. But this "lack of experience" explanation is not sufficient; Robin, as described below, also lacked experience, yet she talked about children in much more organicist terms.

Unlike Chris, Robin pictured children as moving through numerous milestones or landmarks; in this sense she believed in organicist development (Seifert, 1992). Yet her idea of development was universal and inevitable to a fault, as if a child were more an idea or stereotype than a tangible, living creature. Except for a brief mention of her nephew, she never referred to actual individual children. All of her comments were expressed in the present tense, as if she were sharing truths about "the" child that transcended time and space. Like Chris, Robin presumably talked from her (lack of) experience: her readings plus personal memories of her own childhood, neither of which may have highlighted individual variations in developmental pathways.

In naming skills and behaviors as landmarks, Robin made few allowances for variations in their timing or nature. Sometimes the landmarks were relatively accurate, judged by conventional developmental psychology, but other times they sounded like a "fractured" textbook—oddly selected and oddly timed. Consider these examples:

*Language acquisition:* "Learning to talk [is a landmark]. Noticing how people react to your communication. I think that begins to happen about when they're a year old . . . [and concludes] at a year and a half or maybe two years."

*Motor skills:* "By age three they have the ability to focus on objects that pass by. Some kids—I think at three—can hop on one leg. But they can't dance until five."

*Emotions:* "If you really want to know the worst that a child can act, I would say twos and threes. . . . They just have *tempers,* I think. I've never seen a child at two and three that hasn't really had a temper."

*Play:* "[At age five or six] the child's imagination goes pretty wild, and you kind of get a feeling of how they think. . . . They'll tell you, 'Well this is my imaginary friend, and we're playing house.' And they come up with these stories."

*Social development:* "In kindergarten and first grade, friends aren't very close. Children just kind of play together. They don't really know each other. It takes way through grade school before children really talk, really be friends."

Overall, the existence of landmarks seemed more central to Robin's view of "the" child than their organic coherence. Even though she implied social and emotional changes as well as cognitive ones, she left the general impression of childhood as a relatively automatic, even passive, process. For Robin's child there were few developmental dilemmas needing resolution and no obvious transcendence to qualitatively new, more integrated stages of maturity.

## Early Childhood Teachers

Compared to the other groups, diversity was not nearly as characteristic of the descriptions by early childhood teachers. Instead their responses conveyed a remarkably uniform perspective on "the" child, one that was contextualist in Pepper's terms but that, in previous discussions (Seifert and Handziuk, 1993; Seifert, 1994), I have termed *humanistic existentialism.*

Whether named contextualism or humanistic existentialism, the teachers' perspective was marked by three beliefs: that children have an ability to make decisions for themselves; that children are completely unique as individuals; and that children are vulnerable to the vagaries of social circumstance. Unlike Mary Clare, the teachers had a strong belief in "the" child's existence as a separate human entity. Unlike Martha, they expressed a vivid belief that children's futures are uncertain. Unlike Chris, they expressed a belief that "the" child was fundamentally different from an adult. Unlike Robin, they emphasized individual differences among children. And unlike any of the others, the teachers' epistemological commitments were not held individually but in common as a group and consistently as individuals.

The elements of the teachers' contextualism are conveyed by some of their comments.

| Theme | Examples of Comments |
|---|---|
| The child has ability to make decisions. | "I think that [children] create themselves, adapt themselves. . . . in order to survive."—Cheryl |
| | "[Children] can think about what's right and wrong just as well as you and me. We don't give them enough credit."—Darren |
| The child is unique, has a unique history. | "Teachers have so many problems because [kids] are all so individual and need different kinds of motivation. . . . So it's hard to keep track of children."—Jane |
| | "Everybody's unique, and there's no set time for anything. Where and when, and even what [a child] becomes—it's all different."—Bonny |
| The child's future is finite, vulnerable and uncertain. | "A lot depends on the [child's] situation—if you're from a poor family and have to go out and work at fourteen. It all depends, and sometimes things work out better for some people."—Julia |
| | "I think children are very vulnerable because they're smaller physically and don't have any power. I think it's really difficult not to abuse power. . . . and it's important to recognize how easy it is to dominate or control someone who's smaller."—Darren |

Without exception, the eleven early childhood teachers expressed these themes when talking about the nature of particular children or of "the" child. Differences occurred only in the articulation of the sentiments, with novice teachers having less to say than experienced teachers. By contrast, as discussed more fully in the next section, students and parents were eclectic in their thinking, as well as diverse among themselves.

## Everyday Views and Root Metaphors

The teachers in these studies more truly based their thinking on a consistent metaphor than did the parents or students. Judging by their comments, the early childhood teachers regarded "the" child always and foremost as an active, autonomous decision maker, continuously engaged in self-development and in the process of creating a destiny. This view closely resembled Pepper's root metaphor of contextualism: for the early childhood teachers, as for Pepper's contextualist, the world is built around one-of-a-kind events in context. The teachers' comments emphasized both the child's unique choices and the contingency of each child's life course.

Although members of the other groups sometimes also implied support for some sort of contextualism, their commitment to it was more ambiguous and often mixed with competing worldviews. As noted earlier, for example, Mary Clare called attention to the uniqueness of her two children, an action that could be construed as supporting contextualism. At another point, however, she emphasized the similarities between herself and youngsters. Did she do so because she also thought of "the" child in formist terms? Similar ambiguities occurred for Martha. At one point she noted developmental phases that lead to children's self-control. Did this suggest a root metaphor of organicism? Perhaps. But she also talked about children as a type of adult—"little people"—as a formist would, and about specific behaviors (eating, etiquette) that need learning, as a mechanist would.

Likewise, the university students presented metaphorical ambiguities. Chris mostly denied developmental changes (formism?) but also emphasized children's need to take responsibility for their own learning (contextualism?). Robin noted landmarks of development in childhood, as an organicist would, but talked about these in formist terms, as simply descriptions of the type of creature "the" child is. Like the parents, students used root metaphors eclectically, at least during research interviews that inquired about general beliefs.

A sense of the difference between early childhood teachers and the other two groups is conveyed in Table 5.1, which tabulates the diversity of metaphors expressed by all thirty-two participants. Overall, as already explained, teachers relied on just one metaphor (contextualism), but parents and students relied on more than one. The differences are too small to be statistically significant, of course, but they are suggestive of the qualitative trend nonetheless.

**Table 5.1. Diversity of Root Metaphors: Number of Root Metaphors Dominant by Group**

|  | Contextualism | Two | Three | Four |
|---|---|---|---|---|
| Parents (N = 7) | 0 | 2 | 2 | 3 |
| Students (N = 14) | 0 | 6 | 8 | 0 |
| Teachers (N = 11) | 11 | 0 | 0 | 0 |

## Why the Uniformity Among Early Education Teachers?

Why should this pattern have occurred? Why should parents and university students have varied more, both within themselves and among themselves? There are three possible explanations (that are not mutually exclusive): (1) the effects of socialization to roles as parents, students, or teachers; (2) greater self-selection in early childhood teaching; (3) self-presentation of coherence and uniformity.

**Effects of Socialization to Roles as Parents, Students, or Teachers.** The first and most obvious possibility is that parents, students, and teachers differ in socialization to their roles. This possibility is most likely with early childhood teachers because this group has a relatively distinct set of experiences in common—their professional training, which is not shared by students or parents. Could the training lead to common root metaphors of "the" child? The possibility is supported by other studies of early childhood teachers' everyday thinking and children, which also find comparative uniformity in this group (Edwards, Gandini, and Giovaninni, 1996). And it has face validity: the professional literature in early education seems relatively uniform philosophically. Most major publications in early childhood education strongly imply a contextualist worldview. The landmark work of the National Association for the Education of Young Children titled *Developmentally Appropriate Practice for Children Ages 0 to 8* (Bredekamp and Copple, 1997), for example, expresses a contextualist view of the child by recommending that children make choices wherever possible—presumably because each child has unique needs and goals. The contextualist metaphor is echoed in other publications for early childhood teachers, by experienced veterans when they talk about their work, and by workshops intended for the professional development of early childhood teachers.

Socialization into the role of preservice early education student presents a very different picture. Through classes and readings, education students may indeed be exposed to the dominant root metaphors of the early childhood profession. But these exposures have not had many years to exercise their influence yet, and they are in any case interspersed with general socialization to university life, which does not directly relate to beliefs about children.

Overall, these circumstances make it relatively likely that university students would describe their beliefs in more eclectic or "unselected" terms than would experienced teachers of young children.

Socialization into the role of parent presents a more complicated picture because parents are a more numerous and diverse group and because socialization into parenthood spans many years of life. As Lightfoot and Valsiner (1992) have pointed out, parents are normally exposed to a wide range of contradictory messages about appropriate child-rearing goals and practices, messages that often contain contradictory beliefs about the nature of children. Taken as a whole, for example, the parent-advice literature simultaneously emphasizes the uniqueness of each parent's child and the universality of developmental stages (for example, Leach, 1994; Spock and Rothenberg, 1992). It also outlines mechanisms for shaping good behavior yet urges parents to accept the type of child they already have. Collectively, the messages constitute the basis for personal ethnotheories of the child that are conceptually eclectic. The cultural contradictions also create differences among parents by influencing where and from whom individual parents seek advice and support in raising their own particular children (Harkness and Super, 1992).

**Greater Self-Selection in Early Childhood Teaching.** A uniform view of "the" child may be created not only by uniform socialization experiences but also by prior self-selection of individuals into a role. Perhaps, in this case, persons select themselves into early childhood teaching *because* of a relatively common worldview; working with the young may provide a social niche for persons with an ongoing commitment to contextualism.

There is ample support for this possibility among teachers, as well as for the possibility that self-selection operates more weakly among parents and students. As the teacher education literature suggests, an early childhood teacher is a certain sort of person: almost always female, usually middle class, tolerant of working in a gender-conventional occupation, and tolerant of wages even lower than those paid in other female-dominated occupations. Most important, the work itself requires someone willing to focus attention on and value the human potential of relatively undeveloped individuals (Robinson, 1986; Seifert, 1988). These factors create a cohort that ignores (or at least gives up on) "extrinsic" rewards, such as high salary and public recognition, but that values the intrinsic rewards made possible by a contextualist view of childhood. Persons with this perspective would therefore be more likely than others to stay in the profession for extended periods. By the same token, persons new to the profession (like preservice students) might not express the dominant philosophy of the profession consistently; many of them might not know how to do so yet or might have yet to discover that contextualism is not actually a philosophy they prefer.

Compared with motives for becoming an early childhood teacher, motives for becoming a parent are relatively varied and ambiguous (Hamner and Turner, 1996) and may reflect diverse, mutually contradictory cultural beliefs and practices rather than coherent root metaphors about children. As with preservice students, parents may therefore be expected to show diversity of beliefs about the nature of children when they first become parents. Yet self-selection may not operate to reduce the diversity as parents gain experience. Remaining a parent for a child's lifetime does not represent a "choice" in the same sense as remaining an early childhood teacher for one's entire working life: there are cultural sanctions against "resigning" from parenthood that do not apply to teachers. Persons who continue parenting for years, like those described in these studies, are unlikely to do so because they believe in a particular root metaphor of "the" child.

**Self-Presentation of Coherence and Uniformity.** A more psychological interpretation of teachers' uniformity focuses on the interviews themselves as rhetorical events (Mishler, 1986): perhaps individuals reveal only selected images of themselves in interviews, adjusted to the purposes of the interview. Those interviewed in their capacity as early childhood teachers, therefore, will present beliefs about "the" child consistent with this role. The same individuals, if interviewed in their capacity as parents (or nonparents, or anything other than early childhood teachers), might present beliefs about "the" child that are quite different.

In the present studies, in particular, the early childhood teachers may have expressed remarkably uniform views of "the" child because they were playing the role of early childhood educators. The parents and university students were not constrained by a focused role enactment. It is possible, however, that they were guided by a deliberately *un*focused role enactment, such as that of "the casual, untheoretical conversationalist," that could account for an eclectic perspective. Rather different impressions about diversity might have emerged if, for example, all three groups had been cast in other roles. What if all participants, including teachers, were asked to talk about uncertainties and inconsistencies in children's behavior, as if they were psychotherapists? Or what if all were asked to make public recommendations about children's needs, as if they were academic experts? Or to imagine that they were all parents? Without instructions on how to present themselves, parents could have construed their task as "acting like parents"—talking casually and eclectically about their own particular children. Students could have construed theirs as "acting like students"—trying to display whatever (limited) textbook knowledge they have about children in general. And teachers could have construed theirs as "acting professional"—as an advocate of the professionally correct view, one based on contextualism.

## Implications for Knowing and Teaching About "the" Child

Considered as a group, the research reviewed here suggests that parents and students are more diverse or eclectic in their everyday thinking about children and child development than are experienced early childhood teachers and that experienced teachers support a relatively uniform version of contextualism with strong humanistic and existentialist overtones. I have offered speculations about why the teachers in particular were more uniform. These possibilities have a number of implications, both for research and for educational policies concerning parents, students, and early childhood teachers.

**Understanding Constructions of "the" Child.** The outcomes of these studies suggest that we need to understand better the factors or circumstances that create both diversity and uniformity of beliefs. Can they be identified? One way would be to tease apart individuals' self-presentations or roles. Following the methods of the current studies, for example, we might interview persons who normally live multiple roles—persons who were both parents *and* teachers or both students *and* teachers. Dual-role persons were avoided in the earlier research in a deliberate effort to clarify the impact of particular roles. In retrospect this strategy may have failed because it confounded individuals' self-presentations with deeper beliefs that transcend roles and situations. If so, we might learn more from persons who can, for example, speak not only as parents but also as early childhood teachers. Would they express diversity in the first role but uniformity in the second? It would certainly be possible to find out.

**Education of Parents and Teachers.** What do the findings and interpretations mean for educating parents and teachers? The most obvious point is a contextualist one and has been stated elsewhere: that two neighbors, classmates, or colleagues do not necessarily mean the same thing when they both talk of "the" child. Each operates from a different history of experiences—experiences that are constantly reinterpreted and presented anew to others in light of evolving and unique individual circumstances (Kavanaugh, 1989). Discussing children with true mutual understanding requires attending to these differing frameworks. Teachers and parents must understand differing philosophical frameworks in order to avoid mutual dissatisfaction in their encounters (see Chapters Four and Six of this volume).

Furthermore, achieving a mutual philosophical framework poses a different problem for parents or university students than for early childhood teachers. For a group that is already diverse or eclectic (like parents or students), the problem is to create a common framework or meaning for "the" child. Such a group must find a metalanguage or metaphilosophy for discussion, one that will account for as many perspectives and understandings as possible—a common "theory of the child." A group that is relatively uniform (like early childhood teachers), however, already has a common language for discussing children and is challenged instead to appreciate the self-presentational aspect of their discourse—the fact that professionally correct things to say may sometimes obscure deeply held, implicit differences in perspective. Related to this challenge is the need to understand nonprofessional perspectives sympathetically, even if they seem misguided, inconsistent, or even pernicious.

As it turns out, achieving sympathetic understanding of others' root metaphors of "the" child requires a very contextually oriented worldview (Pepper, 1942; Kavanaugh, 1989). The current research suggests that experienced early childhood teachers may already be rather contextually oriented—reassuring news for both parents and leaders in this field. But we still cannot assume that all early childhood teachers think contextually or that they do so in everyday meetings with the public as well as on special occasions with research interviewers.

## References

American Psychiatric Association. *Diagnostic and Prescriptive Statistical Manual—Volume IV*. Washington, D.C.: American Psychiatric Association, 1994.

Bredekamp, S., and Copple, C. (eds.). *Developmentally Appropriate Practice for Children Ages 0 to 8*. Washington, D.C.: National Association for the Education of Young Children, 1997.

Edwards, C. P., Gandini, L., and Giovaninni, D. "The Contrasting Developmental Timetables of Parents and Preschool Teachers in Two Cultural Communities." In S. Harkness and C. M. Super (eds.), *Parents' Cultural Belief Systems: Their Origins, Expressions, and Consequences*. New York: Guilford Press, 1996.

Hamner, T., and Turner, P. *Parenting in Contemporary Society*. (3rd ed.) Needham Heights, Mass.: Allyn & Bacon, 1996.

Harkness, S., and Super, C. M. "Parental Ethnotheories in Action." In I. E. Sigel, A. V. McGillicuddy-DeLisi, and J. J. Goodnow (eds.), *Parental Belief Systems: The Psychological Consequences for Children*. (2nd ed.) Mahwah, N.J.: Erlbaum, 1992.

Harkness, S., Super, C. M., Keefer, C. H., Raghavan, C., and Kipp Campbell, E. "Ask the Doctor: The Negotiation of Cultural Models in the American Parent-Pediatrician Discourse." In S. Harkness and C. M. Super (eds.), *Parents' Cultural Belief Systems: Their Origins, Expressions, and Consequences*. New York: Guilford Press, 1996.

Kavanaugh, P. "William James' Pragmatism: A Clarification of the Contextual World View." In D. Kramer and M. Bopp (eds.), *Transformation in Clinical and Developmental Psychology*. New York: Springer, 1989.

Lakoff, G. *Women, Fire, and Dangerous Things*. Chicago: University of Chicago Press, 1987.

Leach, P. *Children First*. New York: Knopf, 1994.

Lightfoot, C., and Valsiner, J. "Parental Belief Systems Under the Influence: Social Guidance of the Construction of Personal Cultures." In I. E. Sigel, A. V. McGillicuddy-DeLisi, and J. J. Goodnow (eds.), *Parental Belief Systems: The Psychological Consequences for Children*. (2nd ed.) Mahwah, N.J.: Erlbaum, 1992.

Mishler, E. *Research Interviewing: Context and Narrative*. Cambridge, Mass.: Harvard University Press, 1986.

Pepper, S. *World Hypotheses: A Study of Evidence*. Berkeley: University of California Press, 1942.

Robinson, B. "Men Caring for Young Children." In R. Lewis and M. Sussman (eds.), *Men's Changing Roles in the Family*. New York: Haworth Press, 1986.

Seifert, K. "The Culture of Early Education and the Preparation of Male Teachers." *Early Child Development and Care*, 1988, *15*, 35–43.

Seifert, K. "What Develops in Informal Theories of the Child?" *Journal of Learning About Learning*, 1992, 5(1), 3–14.

Seifert, K. "Informal Theories of the Child Among Early Childhood Educators." *Canadian Children*, 1993, 18(2), 21–26.

Seifert, K. "Students' Constructions of Learning and Development." Paper presented at the annual meeting of the Jean Piaget Society, Chicago, June 1994.

Seifert, K., and Handziuk, D. "Informal Ontologies of `the Child.'" Paper presented at the biennial meeting of the Society for Research on Child Development, New Orleans, March 1993.

Spock, B., and Rothenberg, M. *Dr. Spock's Baby and Child Care.* (6th ed.) New York: Dutton, 1992.

*KELVIN L. SEIFERT is professor of educational psychology and early childhood education at the University of Manitoba, Winnipeg, Manitoba, Canada.*

**6**

*Parent-teacher conferences between Latino immigrant parents and their children's elementary school teacher revealed cross-cultural value conflict. Discourse analysis indicated that parents and the teacher often use different criteria to evaluate children's progress; that is, they have different goals for child development. The teacher's goals are usually more individualistic, whereas the parents' goals are often more collectivistic.*

# Cross-Cultural Conflict and Harmony in the Social Construction of the Child

*Patricia Marks Greenfield, Blanca Quiroz, Catherine Raeff*

Adults in a culture symbolically construct an ideal child, and this ideal child is shaped by the culture's goals for child development. However, the nature of this ideal varies from culture to culture (Harkness and Super, 1996). Ethnic diversity therefore implies varying definitions of the ideal child. Many American schools are currently populated by children coming from immigrant families. Insofar as home culture differs from school culture, it is possible that parents and teachers may construct different images of the ideal child. Parent-teacher conferences furnish a uniquely rich and suitable locus for studying the social construction of the child and its variability within a

This research was made possible by a grant from the University of California Linguistic Minority Program. Catherine Raeff was supported by a postdoctoral fellowship from the Applied Developmental Psychology Training Grant, University of California, Los Angeles, Graduate School of Education. Preparation of the final manuscript was supported by the Fogarty International Center of the National Institutes of Health, the Carnegie Corporation, and the Russell Sage Foundation. Special thanks to the teacher and families who participated in the study. Appreciative thanks to Maricela Correa for an excellent job of reliability coding in both Spanish and English. Our appreciation to Elinor Ochs and Alessandro Duranti for their insightful comments on earlier drafts and to Elinor Ochs and Patrick Gonzales for their expert help with transcription. Many thanks to our research assistants, Jacqueline Escobar and Mirella Benitez, for their help in data collection, and to the Greenfield lab group for their formative comments on the earliest drafts. An earlier version of this chapter was presented in "The Social Construction of the Child: Understanding Variability Within and Across Contexts," a symposium (C. M. Super, chair) at the biennial meeting of the Society for Research in Child Development, Indianapolis, March 30, 1995.

context. The conference exemplifies social construction because both parents and teachers are not only evaluating the child but, much more important for our purposes, they are indicating their *criteria* of evaluation—what they think is important in child development.

The whole purpose of such conferences is for parent and teacher to cooperatively construct a symbolic child through the social process of linguistic communication. Sometimes, however, the process of cooperative social construction misfires: because of their differing expectations and goals regarding child development, parent and teacher do not symbolically construct the same child. Their constructions diverge, producing communication difficulties. Both the cooperative and the divergent modes of constructing a symbolic child are revealed through discourse processes. This is the methodological origin of our project.

The social origin of the project is quite different. In the course of starting our exploration of cultural diversity in elementary schools in Los Angeles, we began to hear complaints about lack of communication during parent-teacher conferences from immigrant Latino parents and from their children's teachers. Each group expressed frustration with the other. Neither seemed to understand the underlying causes of the problem.

Paradoxes abounded. For example, one teacher told us that parents were uninterested in their children's academic achievement and often changed the subject to their children's social behavior. Yet, Goldenberg and Gallimore (1995), after a review of the past decade of research, concluded that Latino immigrant families actually desire involvement in their children's education. Furthermore, Latino immigrant parents express a deep and abiding belief that formal education is the means to social and economic mobility (Goldenberg and Gallimore, 1995; Reese, Goldenberg, Loucky, and Gallimore, 1995). We wondered if the resolution of this paradox might lie in contrasting assumptions about the goals of child development (see Harkness and Super, 1996) and education brought to the conference by parents and teachers. We thought we might be able to uncover these contrasting assumptions by looking more carefully at the discourse processes of parent-teacher conferences.

Indeed, there was theoretical reason to believe that immigrant Latino parents and their children's teachers would bring different socialization values to the conference table. Our underlying theoretical rationale was that the range of variation in definitions of the ideal person—the desired endpoints of development—range from the individualistic to the collectivistic. In the former, the ideal is to achieve one's potential for the sake of self-fulfillment and engage in chosen relationships (see Chapter Four of this volume). In the individualistic ideology, one is free to think and act according to personal choice; relationships are ideally egalitarian, based on mutual consent and negotiation (Raeff, 1997). In contrast, the collectivistic ideal is the interdependent person who strives to integrate into the group (most often, the family) by contributing personal abilities and achievements to the social whole. Part of the collectivistic ideal is the obligation to be socially responsive to the group by being responsible for one's own ascribed roles in the group (Greenfield, 1994; Kagitçibasi, 1996; Markus and Kitayama, 1991; Triandis, 1989; Miller, 1994). Although roles are differentiated, each is accorded equal value. Institutions of the United States—including schools—exemplify an individualistic orientation (Raeff, 1997). In contrast, Latino immigrants bring the latter orientation with them from their homelands (Delgado-Gaitan, 1994; García-Coll and Vásquez-García, 1995; Tapia-Uribe, LeVine, and LeVine, 1994; Parke and Buriel, 1998).

Empirically, these differing orientations are reflected in differing views of education and child development. For example, Latino immigrant parents from Mexico and Central America use the Spanish word *educación,* which differs in meaning from its English cognate "education" (Reese, Balzano, Gallimore, and Goldenberg, 1995; Goldenberg and Gallimore, 1995). Discussions of *educación* indicate that, for many Latino immigrants, being "educated" means behaving properly and respectfully, in addition to succeeding academically in school. Indeed, most Latino parents do not separate academic and moral goals for their children (Reese, Balzano, Gallimore, and Goldenberg, 1995).

A similar conception of education is found among Puerto Ricans in Puerto Rico and the United States (Harwood, Miller, and Lucca Irizarry, 1995). For them, the goal of formal education is to construct a "teachable student." In this cultural context *un niño educado* (a well-taught child) is *respetuoso* (respectful), *obediente* (obedient), *tranquilo* (quiet), and *amable* (amiable) (Harwood, Miller, and Lucca Irizarry, 1995).

These collectivistic values can be in conflict, pragmatically, with the goals of educational development in individualistic societies that require a "good student" to work independently, strive for excellent individual achievement, and to engage in skillful self-expression. Although there are individualistic forms of social relationships (see Chapter Four of this volume), parent-teacher conferences generally focus on individual achievement. For this reason they may constitute a setting that is particularly vulnerable to conflict between individualistic and collectivistic values.

Additionally, on the level of particular school activities, the skills that are valued from an individualistic perspective may actually undermine collectivistic developmental goals. For example, teaching logical-rational skills may generate conflict between Latino families and schoolteachers because the latter require children to voice and defend their own opinions. However, for Latino families, emphasis on one's own opinions, especially when they differ from one's parents' views, undermines respect for elders and their ascribed roles (Delgado-Gaitan, 1993, 1994).

Indeed, our earlier research documented that working-class immigrant parents who have come to Los Angeles from Mexico and Central America bring with them an ethnotheory of development that emphasizes collectivistic values (see Chapter Four of this volume). We found that this ethnotheory of development often comes into conflict with the more individualistic views of their children's teachers. In contrast, we found that European American parents generally held to an individualistic ethnotheory of development. This ethnotheory of development was in harmony with that of their children's teachers.

In that research we explored cultural values through *hypothetical* responses to *imaginary* situations. Such responses yield a picture of cultural and individual *ideals* concerning human development. But ideal values are enacted and have their force on the level of everyday interactions. It is through such interactions that basic cultural values are both expressed and instilled. Parent-teacher conferences provide an interactive situation where basic cultural values may be displayed. They bring together parent and teacher ethnotheories of development in an interactive context. Where parents and teachers share common values, there is an opportunity for shared assumptions about the goals of child development. This underlying agreement leads to harmony in the social construction of the child. Where the participants do not share common values, misunderstanding is likely.

## Goals of the Study

The goals of this research are threefold: (1) to present a methodology for identifying cooperation or discord in the interactive construction of the child; (2) to describe the issues in child development that generate cooperative or discordant communication; and thereby (3) to provide a causal analysis of the frustrating communication experienced by Latino immigrant parents and their children's teachers.

**Participants and Procedure.** We videotaped a set of nine naturally occurring parent-teacher conferences between immigrant Latino parents and their children's European American elementary school teachers. All the children came from the same classroom, a third grade–fourth grade combination in a Los Angeles elementary school primarily serving a working-class immigrant Latino population. The teacher was therefore a constant across the nine conferences. Conferences were attended either by the mother, the father, or both parents, as well as the student; sometimes other siblings were present.

The children's parents (not all present at the conferences) had from five to twenty-six years of residence in the United States. Seven couples were born in Mexico, one in El Salvador, and one had a parent from each of the two countries. The educational level of the parents ranged from kindergarten through high school. The modal educational level was sixth grade; in Mexico, family financial hardships and the cost of educational materials often force children to abandon school after sixth grade. In addition, it is the highest level available at all in many rural areas.

**Analysis of the Conferences.** Discourse analysis focuses on the linguistic and paralinguistic *dynamics* and *relationship between speakers* in a conversation (in contrast to content analysis, which focuses on the meaning—*what* is said—as opposed to the interactional dynamics). Discourse analysis was our methodological choice for two reasons: it focuses on inter-actional processes, and it enables the researcher to go beneath the surface of conversational content to examine more basic aspects of the communi-cation process.

Our discourse analysis will focus, in turn, on two different types of dynamics occurring in parent-teacher conferences. In the first, there is implicit agreement on developmental goals. In the second, there is implicit disagree-ment on developmental goals. (Compare Gutierrez, Rymes, and Larson, 1995.)

Following the qualitative analysis of discourse processes, a quantitative analysis will be presented. The goal of the qualitative discourse analysis is to identify the dynamic interactional processes through which larger values are instantiated and enacted on the level of an important conversational event, the parent-teacher conference. The complementary goal of the quantitative analysis is to assess the prevalence of cooperative and noncooperative con-structions of the child in the entire set of parent-teacher conferences.

## Identifying Cooperative Social Construction: Examples of Implicit Agreement on Developmental Goals

Cooperative construction of any topic is manifested in discourse when one party ratifies a topic, confirms a comment, or elaborates on a topic intro-duced by the other party. Any of these communicative moves indicates an uptake of the topic presupposed by the first speaker's conversational move (Ochs Keenan and Schieffelin, 1983). *Ratification of a topic* or *confirmation of a comment* can be verbal, nonverbal, or both; *elaboration* must have a ver-bal component.

We now present examples of such cooperative discourse processes used to interactively construct the child in one of our parent-teacher conferences. A few transcription conventions have been used in transcribing all of the examples in this chapter, as explained below. In addition, punctuation is used to indicate intonation and pausing rather than being used in strict accordance with the rules of grammar.

| *Symbol* | *Explanation* |
|---|---|
| :: | A double colon symbolizes lengthening of a syllable. |
| — | A dash indicates being cut off by the next speaker. |
| = | A pair of equal signs, one after an earlier utterance and one before a later utterance, indicates that the later followed the earlier with no discernible silence between them. |
| (( . . . )) | Material between double parentheses provides information about bodily movement. |
| [ . . . ]<br>[ . . . ] | When brackets are lined up vertically, the material in both sets of brackets was said simultaneously. |

The parents in Examples 1 and 2 are the same couple. Both were born in Mexico; the father has been in the United States for twenty-three years, the mother for twenty years. Both were educated in Los Angeles. The father, who is self-employed in boat maintenance and construction, has an eleventh-grade education; the mother has gone through eighth grade.

### Example 1: Parents Confirm Teacher's Comment About Child

Teacher, mother, father, and Betty (the subject of the conference) are seated at a table in the classroom (conference 9).

1. *Teacher:* ((Pointing to report card)) Takes pride in her work. Most of the time her work is neat, but I'd like her to work a li::ttle bit harder on trying to make sure that just—not perfect, bu[t  a s ]=
2. *Father:*                                              [Yeah.]
3. *Teacher:* =neat as possible
4. *Mother:* Yeah, a little bit—
5. *Teacher:* Yeah, a little neater.
6. *Mother:* Yeah, a little bit neater.
7. *Teacher:* ((Looking at Betty)) Yeah, work on your handwriting a little bit.
8. *Mother:* Yeah, she could improve it.
9. *Teacher:* Yeah, but it's not bad.

Note that in this example, the father first uses the affirmative "Yeah" (turn 2) to express agreement with the teacher; this is a verbal confirmation of a comment. The mother more specifically confirms the teacher's comment (child's work needs to be neater), first through attempting to restate the teacher's comment (turn 4), then through the device of repetition in turn 6, where she repeats almost word for word what the teacher has said in turn 5. The mother gives an even stronger reconfirmation in turn 8 ("Yeah, she could improve it") by extending the teacher's prior comment to her daughter ("work on your handwriting a little bit"). Throughout, the dialogue presupposes an implicit and agreed-upon child development goal: the improvement of Betty's schoolwork.

In the preceding example, the parents confirm comments made by the teacher, mutually reinforcing a shared goal of child development. Harmony concerning shared goals can also be constructed through reversing roles. In the next example, the teacher takes up and elaborates on a topic introduced by the mother.

### Example 2: Teacher Elaborates on Topic Introduced by Mother

Mother has been discussing Betty's difficulty in reading aloud (conference 9).

1. *Mother:* Uh, um, um, I wanted to, you know, if, (short pause) ask your opinion.
2. *Teacher:* Uh-huh.

3. *Mother:* Um, I've been hearing a lot about that "Hooked on Phonics."
4. *Teacher:* Oh, yeah, yeah.
5. *Mother:* And I was wondering you know, if you really know if it, if it works.
6. *Teacher:* Well, I'll tell you something. It depends on how she was taught to read when she was younger.
7. *Mother:* Uh-huh.

The teacher spends four turns elaborating on alternative methods of reading instruction, while the parents periodically agree with "yeah" (three turns).

15. *Teacher:* I think everything has to be done. I think that it's important to let the children have an easy time reading, but how can they read if they don't know the letters? So, I don't know how Betty was taught in the first and second grade *how* to read. But if she wasn't taught with phonics, that program would be very good.

In this example, it is the teacher who not only ratifies the mother's topic (the reading program "Hooked on Phonics") but further validates it through extensive elaboration. Looking at the transcript, we see that the topic of "Hooked on Phonics" is introduced by the mother in turn 3, ratified by the teacher in turn 4, then elaborated by the teacher into a general discussion of methods of reading instruction from turn 6 to turn 15. The point here is not only *what* the teacher says but also *how much* she says: that she thinks the topic is worth saying a lot about. Again, an implicit and agreed-upon child development goal emerges during the dialogue: the improvement of Betty's reading skills.

These two examples make yet another point about the social process of constructing the child in this particular parent-teacher conference: the process is a reciprocal one. Note that in Example 1 the *mother* takes up the *teacher's* topic by confirming her comment, whereas in Example 2 it is the *teacher* who ratifies and expands on a topic that the *mother* has introduced. It is the opportunity for both parties to suggest topics and have them taken up by the other that makes this constructional process not only cooperative but also socially symmetrical.

Before going on to a contrasting example of value *conflict* in the social construction of the child, it is interesting to note that these parents came to the United States from Mexico when they were very young; they were unique in our sample in having had all of their formal education in the United States. This conference, in fact, was the most harmonious of all nine in the cooperative construction of developmental goals. Thus, a common educational background between parents and teachers can be related to shared assumptions about child development.

However, educational background may not be the only reason for harmonious communication in these two examples. Another factor may be that, in each example, discussion revolved around a shortcoming of the child rather than around a strength. It has been proposed that the collectivistic system is more comfortable dealing with deficits (in order to bring a person up to the level of the group) than praising achievements (which raises a person above the group). We will explore this hypothesis through quantitative analysis later in the chapter.

## Identifying Noncooperative Discourse: Examples of Implicit Disagreement on Developmental Goals

Noncooperative discourse is signaled when one party fails to ratify the other party's topic. Conversational noncooperation becomes conversational divergence when one partner not only fails to ratify but also changes the other partner's discourse topic. Divergence escalates to discord when the first partner refuses to give up his or her original topic or gives it up with difficulty. The following example illustrates such escalating noncooperation, divergence, and discord between parent and teacher. As will be seen, each party ignores the other party's symbolic construction of child development.

The father in Example 3 began his education in El Salvador, where he was born. He completed his education in Los Angeles, where he currently works as a furniture salesperson.

### Example 3: Escalation of Communication Problems Between Parent and Teacher

Teacher, father, Mira (the subject of the conference), and younger brother are seated at a table in the classroom (conference 6).

1. *Teacher:* She's doing great. She's doing beautifully in English and in reading. *And* in writing, *and* in speaking.
2. *Father:* ((looks down at lap))
3. *Teacher:* It's wonderful.
4. *Father:* ((turning to point to younger son)) The same, this guy, h[e]
5. *Teacher:* (interrupting, with shrill tone) [G]o::od! [He's doing too?]
6. *Father:*                                    [He      can]
   write—
7. *Teacher:* He can write in English?
8. *Father:* Well, his name.
9. *Boy:* ((turns away))
10. *Teacher:* He can write his name?
11. *Father:* Yeah.
12. *Teacher:* That's great!
13. *Boy:* ((turns away))
14. *Teacher:* How old is he?
15. *Father:* Four years old.

Further discussion of the younger brother occupies conversational turns 16–19.

20. *Teacher:* (to younger brother) That's great. (shrill, exaggerated tone) You know how to write your name already—that's wonderful! ((looking down at grades)) (returning to normal tone of voice, as she returns to original topic) Well, so she's doing beautifully.

Teacher goes on for a number of utterances about Mira's improvement in oral expression. Father says nothing, simply nodding politely and offering one affirmative "uh-huh."

In this example, the teacher initiates Mira as a topic (turn 1), commenting on her academic excellence. The father does not cooperate by ratifying this topic. Instead, using a pointing gesture in turn 4, he initiates a new topic, his younger son; this is a divergent conversational move. He continues the divergence by commenting on his son's skills in turns 4, 6, and 8. The teacher ratifies this new topic by confirming the father's comments in turns 5 and 7, but begrudgingly: her interruption (turns 5 and 7) and shrillness (turns 5 and 20) both bespeak her impatience and discomfort with the new topic. The conversational dynamics have escalated to discord. The discord continues when, at the end of turn 20, she, in a normal, much calmer voice, returns the topic to Mira, saying of her, "Well, so she's doing beautifully."

Just as concordant goals were implicit in Examples 1 and 2, so discordant goals are implicit in Example 3. Neither party seems comfortable with the goal of the other. The father shows discomfort when the teacher recognizes his daughter as outstanding, as she does in turn 1; he responds by looking down at his lap in turn 2. According to our analysis, her recognition may threaten the collectivistic goal of integrating each child as an equal contributing part of the family group. Hence, when the teacher symbolically constructs his daughter as an outstanding individual learner, the father implicitly *reconstructs* her as a normative part of the family group by equating her academic skills to those of her younger brother (turns 4, 6, and 8). Note also the lack of recognition of any communication problem throughout the conversation itself.

The father's goal of relating Mira to others in the family is confirmed by a similar switch of topic (after the transcribed segment in Example 3). After the teacher says of Mira, "She's doing very well," the father symbolically relates her to the family group once more, this time by talking of his older daughter and how she helps Mira with her reading homework.

The problem of misunderstanding is not merely a question of language. Both this conference and the conference illustrating shared understanding in the construction of the child (Examples 1 and 2) took place in English. Other parent-teacher conferences in our sample took place in Spanish or in a mixture of Spanish and English, some with the help of a native Spanish-speaking aide as an interpreter. Most often and most fundamentally, the problems stem less from different languages and more from different value systems guiding child development. In conference 8, for instance, the use of Spanish did not prevent the sort of miscommunication illustrated in Example 3.

Conference 8 involved a mother who received a sixth-grade education in Mexico; she had been in the United States for seven years. In the course of this conference, after discussing book report assignments, the teacher asked the mother (in Spanish) if she had any questions. The mother answered, "*No, ninguna—sola que se portaba bien*" ("No, none—only that she was behaving well"). A divergent communication process ensued. The teacher answered the question with a dismissive "*Si, si,*" then changed the topic. Whereas the question was about correct behavior, the teacher commented in Spanish, "*En clase, ella participa. En esta clase, es importante que los alumnos participa oralemente*" (In class, she participates. In this class, it is important that the students participate orally). With her answer, the teacher transformed a question about proper behavior into one about verbal self-expression.

This Spanish-language conference exemplifies a major frustration described in the introduction: the teacher wants to talk about academics; the parent is more concerned about social behavior. However, it is more than a disagreement about priorities. The teacher is encouraging behavior—verbal self-expression—that is considered negative in the parents' cultural framework. Conference 6 (in English) was very revealing in this regard.

In conference 6, when the teacher asked if the father (the same father as in the escalating miscommunication of Example 3) had any questions toward the end of the conference, his reply was, "How is she doing? She don't talk too much?" Clearly, in requesting more talking from the child, the teacher elicited behavior that was considered positive in school but negative according to the community she was teaching. This can create a conflict for both parent and child, and this type of conflict has the potential to alienate children from their parents or from the school. Similarly, it could alienate parents from their children or from their children's school.

These misunderstandings indicate a significant problem in cross-cultural communication: the teacher assumes the importance of self-expression, in line with an individualistic conception of child development; the parent assumes the importance of socially responsible behavior, in line with a collectivistic conception of child development. These different assumptions about classroom behavior may then lead to frustrations with the communication process on both sides.

## Quantitative Analysis

We used eight of the nine videotaped conferences as the basis for the quantitative analysis. The ninth conference was essentially a conversation between the child and the teacher, with the mother, who was also a classroom aide, looking on. Because it contained almost no parent-teacher inter-action, we did not use it in the analyses. We based the quantitative cate-gories on points of conflict that emerged from the qualitative analysis and from review of all nine tapes. The categories were

- Child's individual accomplishment
- Family accomplishment or contribution
- Praise for the child
- Criticism of the child
- Child's cognitive skills
- Child's social skills
- Child's oral expression
- Child's respect for authority
- Advice on parenting role
- Parents teaching their child at home

These categories are elaborated below in the descriptions of the quantita-tive results.

**Reliability.** Two researchers coded every tape. We based interrater reli-ability on a minute-by-minute analysis of initial agreements and disagree-ments between the raters. The two coders resolved disagreements by reviewing the tapes together and deciding on the best code. For agreement to be counted, coders had to agree on when the discourse was relevant (or irrelevant) to a particular category and whether reference to the category elicited cooperative (harmonious) or noncooperative (conflictual) dis-course. Because there was no limit on how many categories could be coded in each unit of time, each category was independent of the others. Based on each minute as a unit, interrater reliability was high, ranging from 0.94 (for cognitive skill) to 1.00 (for individual accomplishment). These levels con-trast sharply with the chance level of agreement of 0.33. Note, too, that these reliability figures include agreement on both the category and the response (cooperative or noncooperative).

**Results.** Cooperative social construction, or agreement on develop-mental goals, occurred less often than conflict and disagreement overall in this sample. Noncooperative discourse occurred in relation to all of the cat-egories. There were 143 instances of noncooperative discourse in these categories and 53 instances of cooperative discourse. In other words, the ratio of noncooperative to cooperative discourse on these key topics was almost three to one. We now take up the individual categories, organized as pairs of conflicting values.

*Individual Versus Family Accomplishment.* We tested the frequency of the value conflict that emerged in Example 3—focus on individual achieve-ment versus focus on family achievement or activity—in the eight parent-teacher conferences that were analyzed. We found that this type of conflict occurred nine times, in a total of five of the eight conferences. In all but one case, the teacher's criterion for positive development was individual accomplishment; the parents' criterion was the accomplishment of the family as a whole or the child's contribution to family accomplishment.

*Praise Versus Criticism.* The harmony in Example 1 of the qualitative analysis occurred in response to a critical comment, whereas the discord in Example 3 occurred in response to praise. We therefore explored the hypothesis that the collectivistic system highlights the value of criticism as a feedback mechanism, whereas the individualistic system highlights the value of praise (Greenfield and Suzuki, 1998). Many collectivistic communities favor criticism to encourage normative behavior, while avoiding praise (Childs and Greenfield, 1980), which may single out a particular child (Markus and Kitayama, 1991).

The avoidance of praising has a particular cultural meaning (see, for example, Appadurai, 1990). U.S. schools are very concerned with maintaining the self-esteem of the child as a learner through maximizing positive (praise) and minimizing negative (critical) feedback. This is an individualistic position because it focuses on how individuals feel about themselves in relation to their own personal achievements. We therefore hypothesized that the teacher's critical comments concerning the child would lead to more cooperative conversation with parents than her positive comments would.

Indeed, criticism elicited more cooperative responses from the parents than did praise (eight cooperative responses to criticism, five cooperative responses to praise). Conversely, praise elicited more noncooperative responses than did criticism (twenty-seven noncooperative responses to praise, eighteen noncooperative responses to criticism). This trend follows the dynamics identified in the qualitative analysis. Even though the parents in conference 9 were educated in the United States, they followed the collectivistic pattern concerning praise and criticism.

Clearly, however, this relationship was a trend rather than an all-or-none pattern. Perhaps a stronger (and unexpected) pattern in these data is the overall tendency for noncooperative responses on the part of parents to evaluative comments (both positive and negative) about their children from the teacher. This pattern is probably based on the value of accepting rather than evaluating family members.

*Cognitive Versus Social Skills.* As illustrated in our earlier example from conference 8 and from our informal interviews with the teacher, parents were typically more interested in issues relevant to their children's social behavior, whereas the teacher was more interested in issues of cognitive development. From this we would predict noncooperative responses to the teacher's topic of cognitive skills. Indeed, noncooperative responses were more frequent (nineteen noncooperative versus fifteen cooperative) when the teacher discussed cognitive skills. It is important to mention here that eight out of the fifteen cooperative responses came from the same conference, the harmonious conference illustrated in Examples 1 and 2; recall that these were the only parents in the sample to have received all of their education in the United States.

On the other hand, cooperative responses slightly predominated (five cooperative versus four noncooperative) when the teacher or parent introduced the topic of social skills. This result agrees with prior research findings that noncognitive aspects of intelligence seem to be more important than cognitive aspects for Mexican immigrant parents (Okagaki and Sternberg, 1993). Again, it is clearly a question of emphasis, not an all-or-none matter.

There was, for example, an unexpected level of noncooperative response on the part of parents when the teacher brought up social skills. The explanation seemed to be that many of these examples came from the behavior section of the report card and involved social behavior that would not be evaluated in the same way by the parents. For example, talking to other students in class was brought up as a form of negative social behavior by the teacher. However, it would not necessarily be seen as negative by the parents, who might, from a more collectivistic perspective, view this form of behavior as a way to strengthen social ties among the class members.

*Oral Expression Versus Respect for Authority.* This contrast is closely related to the prior one: oral expression is considered by the teacher to be a cognitive skill, whereas respect for authority is considered by many parents to be an important aspect of social behavior. In all eight parent-teacher conferences, there were instances when the teacher told the parents that she valued oral language skills or wanted the children to talk more in class. Twenty-six out of the twenty-eight parent responses were noncooperative.

Concerning respect for authority, in four cases a parent expressed worry about behavior that might be interpreted as disrespectful to the teacher, including fear that a child might be talking too much. This pattern indicates that the collectivistic goals of child development in the ancestral culture mandate that it is more appropriate for children to listen to authority figures than to display knowledge through talking in their presence.

*Parenting Role Versus Teaching Role.* Another source of cross-cultural conflict was that the teacher advocated teaching by the parents at home. Parents did not confirm such suggestions, responding with noncooperative conversational moves twenty-one out of twenty-two times. In fact, all the parents (except the parents in Examples 1 and 2) acted as if teaching cognitive skills is up to the teacher at school.

Although the parents did not want to teach at home, they did want to maintain their jurisdiction as socializing agents at home. In seven different conferences, parents responded one or more times with a noncooperative move when the teacher tried to give parents advice on parenting skills. Most parents seemed to believe that parenting is up to the parents at home.

Thus, there was disagreement between parents and teachers concerning the social construction of the actual child. Perhaps these Latino immigrant parents prefer to socialize their children in their own way at home because of a sense that the teacher's suggestions undermine rather than support their ideal child. Perhaps they prefer not to engage in cognitive teaching at home because of their lack of direct experience with the U.S. educational system and limited schooling in their homelands. This latter is probably a major reason why Mexican immigrant parents rely more on older siblings to help their children with schoolwork than European American parents do (Azmitia and others, 1994).

## Conclusions

An important substantive finding of this study is that many differences between parents and teachers in their criteria for child development derive from differences between two implicit cultural models (Harkness and Super, 1996). The teacher's model is of the child as an independent, academic achiever with high self-esteem. The parents' model is of the child as a member of the family, sharing academic skills with others in the family, developing social responsibility, and displaying respectful behavior appropriate to the role of student.

The discord in the conferences also reflects different models of teaching and parenting. The teacher has a model of herself as teaching parents how to teach their children at home. She sees parents as auxiliary teachers, helping the child to succeed academically. The parents, in contrast, have a model of the teacher as their children's sole academic instructor and themselves as the authority on social development at home. Therefore, the teacher encounters resistance to her suggestions that parents teach at home. The parents, in turn, encounter resistance to their suggestions that each party has an exclusive domain of operation: teacher at school, parent at home.

However, discord between the parents and teacher was far from inevitable. Clearly, both communication and miscommunication have been accomplished by one and the same teacher in our study. This range of communicative fit between teacher and parents is a large one. Our hypothesis is that the range would be smaller, the average fit better, if all the pupils were children of parents who had grown up in the United States. If they were, there would be greater basic agreement that the goal of development (and the main point of the parent-teacher conference) is the growth of the child as an individual.

Herein lies our explanation regarding the complaints about communication that we have heard from Latino immigrant parents and from their children's teachers. For many immigrant Latino parents, the lack of understanding of the individualistic worldview impedes agreement on such educational goals. Similarly, teachers' lack of acknowledgment of collectivistic goals of development obstructs their communication with parents and the implicit goal of cooperatively constructing a child.

Given the multicultural environment in which we live, our research has definite social implications. The social policy goal of our research is to help parents and teachers negotiate cultural differences in a positive way, by making them aware of the differing ethnotheory each party may bring to the literal table in cross-cultural parent-teacher conferences, in particular, and to the figurative table in multicultural schooling more generally.

Perhaps most practical as a remedy for cross-cultural miscommunication and the alienation it breeds would be for teachers to acknowledge the price of acculturation. This price, rarely if ever discussed at school or in society at large, is paid when valued goals of child development—such as respect for elders—must be given up in the name of academic achievement. In addition, increased awareness on the part of immigrant families of the basic value differences is needed. It may also be useful to move toward integrating aspects of individualism and collectivism so that both parents' and teachers' goals are valued in school settings.

## References

Appadurai, A. "Topographies of the Self: Praise and Emotion in Hindu India." In C. A. Lutz and L. Abu-Lughod (eds.), *Language and the Politics of Emotion.* Cambridge: Cambridge University Press, 1990.

Azmitia, M., Cooper, C. R., Garcia, E. E., Ittel, A., Johanson, B., Lopez, E. M., Martinez-Chavez, R., and Rivera, L. "Links Between Home and School Among Low-Income Mexican-American and European-American Families." National Center for Research on Cultural Diversity and Second Language Learning, 1994.

Childs, C. P., and Greenfield, P. M. "Informal Modes of Learning and Teaching: The Case of Zinacanteco Weaving." In N. Warren (ed.), *Studies in Cross-Cultural Psychology.* Vol. 2. London: Academic Press, 1980.

Delgado-Gaitan, C. "Parenting in Two Generations of Mexican-American Families." *International Journal of Psychology*, 1993, *16,* 409–427.

Delgado-Gaitan, C. "Socializing Young Children in Mexican-American Families: An Intergenerational Perspective." In P. M. Greenfield and R. R. Cocking (eds.), *Cross-Cultural Roots of Minority Child Development.* Mahwah, N.J.: Erlbaum, 1994.

García-Coll, C., and Vásquez-García, H. A. "Hispanic Children and Their Families: On a Different Track from the Very Beginning." In H. E. Fitzgerald, B. M. Lester, and B. Zuckerman (eds.), *Children of Poverty: Research, Health, and Policy Issues.* New York: Garland, 1995.

Goldenberg, C., and Gallimore, G. "Immigrant Latino Parents' Values and Beliefs About Their Children's Education: Continuities and Discontinuities Across Cultures and Generations." In P. Pintrich and M. Maehr (eds.), *Advances in Achievement Motivation.* Vol. 9. Greenwich, Conn.: JAI Press, 1995.

Greenfield, P. M. "Independence and Interdependence as Developmental Scripts: Implication for Theory, Research, and Practice." In P. M. Greenfield and R. R. Cocking (eds.), *Cross-Cultural Roots of Minority Child Development.* Mahwah, N.J.: Erlbaum, 1994.

Greenfield, P. M., and Suzuki, L. "Culture and Human Development: Implications for Parenting, Education, Pediatrics, and Mental Health." In I. E. Sigel and K. A. Renninger (eds.), *Handbook of Child Psychology* (5th ed.), Vol. 4: *Child Psychology in Practice.* New York: Wiley, 1998.

Gutierrez, K., Rymes, B., and Larson, J. "Script, Counterscript, and Underlife in the Classroom: James Brown Versus *Brown v. Board of Education.*" *Harvard Educational Review,* 1995, *65,* 445–471.

Harkness, S., and Super, C. M. (eds.), *Parents' Cultural Belief Systems: Their Origins, Expressions, and Consequences.* New York: Guilford Press, 1996.

Harwood, R. L., Miller, J. G., and Lucca Irizarry, N. *Culture and Attachment: Perceptions of the Child in Context.* New York: Guilford Press, 1995.

Kagitçibasi, Ç. *Family and Human Development Across Cultures: A View from the Other Side.* Mahwah, N.J.: Erlbaum, 1996.

Markus, H. M., and Kitayama, S. "Culture and the Self: Implications for Cognition, Emotion, and Motivation." *Psychological Review,* 1991, *98,* 224–253.

Miller, J. G. "Cultural Psychology: Bridging Disciplinary Boundaries in Understanding the Cultural Grounding of Self." In P. K. Bock (ed.), *Handbook of Psychological Anthropology.* Westport, Conn.: Greenwood, 1994.

Ochs Keenan, E., and Schieffelin, B. B. "Topic as a Discourse Notion: A Study of Topic in the Conversations of Children and Adults." In E. Ochs Keenan and B. B. Schieffelin, *Acquiring Conversational Competence.* London: Routledge, 1983.

Okagaki, L., and Sternberg, R. J. "Parental Beliefs and Children's School Performance." *Child Development,* 1993, *64,* 36–56.

Parke, R. D., and Buriel, R. "Socialization in the Family: Ethnic and Ecological Perspectives." In W. Damon (series ed.), *Handbook of Child Psychology* (5th ed.), Vol. 3: N. Eisenberg (volume ed.), *Social, Emotional, and Personality Development.* New York: Wiley, 1998.

Raeff, C. "Individuals in Relationships: Cultural Values, Children's Social Interactions, and the Development of an American Individualistic Self." *Developmental Review,* 1997, *17,* 205–238.

Reese, L., Balzano, S., Gallimore, R., and Goldenberg, C. "The Concept of *Educación:* Latino Family Values and American Schooling." *International Journal of Educational Research,* 1995, *23,* 57–81.

Reese, L., Goldenberg, C., Loucky, J., and Gallimore, R. "Ecocultural Context, Cultural Activity, and Emergent Literacy: Sources of Variation in Home Literacy Experiences of Spanish-Speaking Children." In S. W. Rothstein (ed.), *Class, Culture, and Race in American Schools: A Handbook.* Westport, Conn.: Greenwood Press, 1995.

Tapia Uribe, F.M.T., LeVine, R. A., and LeVine, S. E. "Maternal Behavior in a Mexican Community: The Changing Environments of Children." In P. M. Greenfield and R. R. Cocking (eds.), *Cross-Cultural Roots of Minority Child Development.* Mahwah, N.J.: Erlbaum, 1994.

Triandis, H. C. "Cross-Cultural Studies of Individualism and Collectivism." *Nebraska Symposium on Motivation,* 1989, *37,* 41–134.

PATRICIA MARKS GREENFIELD *is professor of psychology at the University of California, Los Angeles.*

BLANCA QUIROZ *received her master's degree in Latin American studies from the University of California, Los Angeles. She is now a doctoral student in human development at Harvard University.*

CATHERINE RAEFF *is a former postdoctoral fellow in applied developmental psychology at the University of California, Los Angeles. She is now assistant professor of psychology at Indiana University of Pennsylvania.*

# INDEX

LeVine, S. E., 73, 74, 95, 108
Lewis, C. C., 12, 19
Lightfoot, C., 42, 56, 88, 91
Logical-rational skills, 95, 104–105
Loucky, J., 108
Lovingness, 47
Lucca Irizarry, N., 43, 44, 46–48, 51, 52, 56, 95, 108
Lutz, C. A., 43, 57

Madsen, M., 70, 74
Marin, G., 13, 19
Markus, H. R., 5, 11, 19, 60, 74, 95, 104, 108
Mechanism (root metaphor): defined, 76; in parental view of child as autonomous creature, 81, 86
Mednick, M., 6, 19
Mernissi, F., 9, 19
Mervielde, I., 28, 39
Metalanguage, 90
Metaphors. *See* Root metaphors
Miller, J. G., 43, 44, 46–48, 51, 52, 56, 62, 65, 74, 95, 108
Miller, P. J., 41, 46, 56
Mills, C. W., 7, 19
Mines, M., 7, 8–9, 19, 49, 56
Mischel, W., 49, 56
Mishler, E., 89, 91
Mistry, J., 41, 55, 56
Miura, K., 12, 18
Moral concepts, 10–11
Mosier, C., 41, 55, 56
Mother-infant interactions: of Puerto Rican versus Anglo American mothers, 52–54; socialization goals and, 52–54; videotaping of, 52
Murkoff, H. E., 50, 56
Muslim Arab societies, personal goals in, 9

National Association for the Education of Young Children, 87
National group membership, 44–46; as cultural community, 49; parental beliefs and, 54–55; socioeconomic status and, 44–46, 49
Netherlands: concepts of dependence in, 30–34, 36–37; concepts of independence in, 34–37; parental descriptions of their children in, 25–37; parental ethnotheories in, study of, 24–38
Nucci, L. P., 10, 11, 12, 19, 49, 56

Obedience. *See* Authority and obedience
Ochs, E., 41, 57, 104
Ochs Keenan, E., 97, 108
Okagaki, L., 105, 108
Ontological dimension, 78, 80
Oral expression versus respect for authority, 105
Organicism (root metaphor): defined, 76–77; in parental view of child, 81–82, 86; in university students' view of child, 82–84
Overton, W., 6, 19

Pachter, L. M., 50, 56
Parental descriptions of their children, 2; American and Dutch, 25–27; cultural concepts of dependence and, 30–34, 36–37; cultural models of the child in, 25–27, 30–37; diversity versus uniformity in, 78–82, 86–87; individualism versus sociocentrism in, 25–30, 37–38; individualistic descriptors in, 28, 29; parental educational level and, 29–30; parent-role socialization and, 87–88; positive and negative frameworks of, 27–28; quantitative analysis of, 27–30; root metaphors in, 78–82, 88–89; significance of independence and, 34–37; sociocentric descriptors in, 28–30
Parental ethnotheories/cultural belief systems, 24; defined, 24; socioeconomic status and, 44–49; uniformity and diversity in, 78–82, 86–87; in United States, of Anglo and Puerto Rican mothers, 46–49; in United States and Netherlands, 24–38
Parenting role: socialization into, 87–88; teaching role versus, as source of cross-cultural conflict, 105–106
Parent-teacher conferences, 2, 75, 93–107; categories of cultural value conflict in, 103–106; cooperative social construction in, 97–100; discourse analysis of, 96–97; implicit agreement on developmental goals in, 97–100; implicit disagreement on developmental goals in, 100–102; Latinos in, 94–107; as locus for study of social constructions of the child, 93–94; noncooperative social construction in, 100–102; quantitative analysis of, 97, 102–106; recommendations for cross-cultural communication in, 106–107; study of, 96–107

# Back Issue/Subscription Order Form

Copy or detach and send to:
**Jossey-Bass Inc., Publishers, 350 Sansome Street, San Francisco, CA 94104-1342**

Call or fax toll free!
**Phone 888-378-2537 6AM–5PM PST; Fax 800-605-2665**

Back issues: Please send me the following issues at $25 each
(Important: please include series initials and issue number, such as CD88)

1. CD _____

_____

_____

$ _____ Total for single issues

$ _____ Shipping charges (for single issues *only;* subscriptions are exempt
from shipping charges): Up to $30, add $5$^{50}$ • $30$^{01}$–$50, add $6$^{50}$
$50$^{01}$–$75, add $7$^{50}$ • $75$^{01}$–$100, add $9 • $100$^{01}$–$150, add $10
Over $150, call for shipping charge

Subscriptions  Please ❏ start  ❏ renew my subscription to *New Directions
for Child and Adolescent Development* for the year _____ at the
following rate:

❏ Individual $67  ❏ Institutional $115
**NOTE:** Subscriptions are quarterly, and are for the calendar year only.
Subscriptions begin with the spring issue of the year indicated above.
For shipping outside the U.S., please add $25.

$ _____ Total single issues and subscriptions (CA, IN, NJ, NY, and DC
residents, add sales tax for single issues. NY and DC residents must
include shipping charges when calculating sales tax. NY and Canadian
residents only, add sales tax for subscriptions.)

❏ Payment enclosed (U.S. check or money order only)
❏ VISA, MC, AmEx, Discover Card # _____ Exp. date _____

Signature _____ Day phone _____
❏ Bill me (U.S. institutional orders only. Purchase order required)
Purchase order # _____

Name _____

Address _____

_____

_____

Phone _____ E-mail _____

For more information about Jossey-Bass Publishers, visit our Web site at:
www.josseybass.com **PRIORITY CODE = ND1**

ERRATUM

NEW DIRECTIONS FOR CHILD AND ADOLESCENT DEVELOPMENT, no. 86, Winter 1999 © Jossey-Bass Publishers

The order of editors' names, as listed on the cover, title page, and copyright page of this volume, was incorrect. The correct order follows:

# Paul D. Hastings, Caroline C. Piotrowski